Strategies for
K–8 Inquiry-Based Learning

Integrating Language Arts and Social Studies

Leah M. Melber, PhD
Museum Education Consultant

Alyce Hunter, PhD
Wagner College

Los Angeles | London | New Delhi
Singapore | Washington DC

Special thanks to Linda and Bill, the ever-supportive Crysta and Janet, and of course, Cordelia, who is always willing to get right in the middle of things and help.

—Leah

Special thanks to all my family for their constant encouragement and particularly to my daughters, Alyson and Jessica, for their perpetual nagging to "get it done."

—Alyce

For information:

SAGE Publications, Inc.
2455 Teller Road
Thousand Oaks, California 91320
E-mail: order@sagepub.com

SAGE Publications Ltd.
1 Oliver's Yard
55 City Road
London EC1Y 1SP
United Kingdom

SAGE Publications India Pvt. Ltd.
B 1/I 1 Mohan Cooperative Industrial Area
Mathura Road, New Delhi 110 044
India

SAGE Publications Asia-Pacific Pte. Ltd.
33 Pekin Street #02-01
Far East Square
Singapore 048763

Printed in the United States of America

Library of Congress Cataloging-in-Publication Data

Melber, Leah M.
Integrating language arts and social studies: 25 strategies for K–8 inquiry-based learning/Leah M. Melber, Alyce Hunter.
    p. cm.
Includes bibliographical references and index.
ISBN 978-1-4129-7110-2 (pbk.)

 1. Language arts (Elementary) 2. Social studies—Study and teaching (Elementary) 3. Inquiry-based learning. I. Hunter, Alyce. II. Title.

LB1576.M438 2010
372.6′044—dc22   2009021459

Printed on acid-free paper

09 10 11 12 13 10 9 8 7 6 5 4 3 2 1

Acquiring Editor:	Diane McDaniel
Editorial Assistant:	Ashley Conlon
Production Editor:	Sarah K. Quesenberry
Copy Editor:	Julie Gwin
Proofreader:	Jennifer Gritt
Typesetter:	C&M Digitals (P) Ltd.
Cover Designer:	Gail Buschman
Marketing Manager:	Christy Guilbault

Contents

Preface

The idea for this book came to me after a brief discussion with a student in my elementary science methods class. She had learned I would be her professor for social studies methods the following quarter and approached me after class to let me know she was looking forward to the course. It was an offhand comment she made as she was walking away that started the planning process: "We probably won't have as much hands-on or inquiry-based learning though. You know, because it's social studies." That's when I realized there was a great opportunity to share a very different approach to social studies than what most of us experienced when we were students.

As a third-grade teacher, I too had spent time in the "textbook trap." It was only after I had the opportunity to observe social science researchers at work that I discovered a better path to social studies instruction. As I had the opportunity to listen to lectures from researchers studying cultures or watch a historian carefully archiving documents central to the development of our city, I developed a better sense of what social studies is. The topic I once disliked as a student myself had now become something of which I couldn't get enough. I also quickly became aware that the practice of using textbook essay questions to retain a tie to language arts skills was unnecessary. The reading of primary sources, writing of analyses, and oral discussion of controversial topics was already a natural part of social science research. I realized then that by creating social studies activities in line with the engaging work of researchers and historians, moving away from a craft or true/false worksheet focus, it was possible I could spark the same excitement in children and, at the same time, provide them with authentic experiences in language arts. With this book in hand, I'm confident you'll feel equally as confident. This book is a collection of strategies I believe to be especially effective in engaging students in active, inquiry-based experiences. It is an attempt to parallel the work of social scientists while still retaining pragmatic elements that are critical for successful implementation in elementary and middle-school classrooms. I'm sure most educators would agree that this is not an easy balancing act! However, it is one that can be managed with inquiry-based social studies instruction complete with hands-on experiences. And although a single classroom lesson cannot fully capture all the richness of a career in the social sciences, it is my hope that these strategies will at least move students closer to a better understanding of these dedicated researchers' work.

I hope that educators at all stages of their career will find something helpful in this publication. The experienced teacher who is already using an inquiry-based approach is likely to find several strategies that he or she hasn't yet tried. For a beginning teacher in his or her first year of teaching, there are activities that require few materials and can be implemented with a minimum of advanced planning. I personally feel that to share this work with preservice teachers is an opportunity for them to view social studies instruction through the lens of inquiry from the very beginning.

A LOOK INSIDE

The book is comprised of five units, each with a central theme. These themes are:

Unit I: Building Research Skills

Unit II: Connecting to Community

Unit III: Multiple Voices

Unit IV: Past and Present

Unit V: Understanding Our World

Each unit includes five different strategies related to each theme. Units and strategies can be used in any order that the reader feels best supports his or her instruction.

Each unit begins with an **overview and rationale** for the theme presented in the strategies that follow.

Each strategy begins with a short **vignette** to provide the reader with view of the strategy in use. The vignette is followed by the **theoretical framework** that summarizes the research base and provides a rationale for strategy use. **Key themes** are then highlighted, and they identify the processes that are at the focus of this particular strategy. These are followed by a **materials list**. A general **overview of the procedures** comes next, and it provides the reader with a broad explanation of strategy implementation. Three sections follow that provide guidance on **modifications** to the general procedure that will make the strategy more appropriate for a particular grade-level range.

Because most teachers work with a diverse student body, additional information on modification options is also provided. When working with **students with special needs**, educators are already well aware that individualized instruction is critical. The generalized modifications presented for working with students with special needs should be seen as a starting point rather than an exhaustive list of intervention strategies. A similar approach should be taken when reviewing the modifications suggested for **English-language learners**. Any protocols that may be specific to your school or district can be used in alignment with these suggestions.

Most of the strategies also have boxes that provide additional support for using each strategy. These boxes highlight relevant **children's literature, sources for unique materials**, as well as special **safety considerations**. Each strategy also provides the reader with a suggested **assessment plan** and sample **scoring rubric** that can be easily modified. Figures of sample **data sheets** or student work examples conclude each strategy and provide the busy educators with the materials to get started right away. Because we know linking to standards is critical, we have also listed Standards for English Language Arts (National Council of Teachers of English and International Reading Association, 1996) and Curriculum Standards for Social Studies (National Council for the Social Studies [NCSS], 1994) that are an especially good match for each strategy. For a full listing of the Standards for the English Language Arts, see p. xi.)

Each strategy is accompanied by suggested methods of incorporating technology. Some include **Web sites** to enhance your instruction. Although it cannot be guaranteed that all Web sites will be functional for years to come, significant care was taken to select established Web sites that are likely to have a continued and reliable presence.

This book is being published during an exciting time in the field of social studies. At press time, the National Council for the Social Studies was still finalizing the newest version of its national standards for social studies education. You will find the current version of individual, relevant social studies standards printed alongside each strategy. When the new versions are published, you will be able to access the updated National Council for the Social Studies standards at **www.sagepub.com/lmelberstudy.**

The current version of the standards has been used with permission from National Council for the Social Studies, *Expectations of Excellence: Curriculum Standards for Social Studies* (NCSS, 1994). This book may be purchased by calling 800–683–0812. Electronic copies of it are not available.

REFERENCES

National Council for the Social Studies. (1994). *Expectations of excellence: Curriculum standards for social studies*. Washington, DC: Author.

National Council of Teachers of English and International Reading Association. (1996). *Standards for the English language arts*. Urbana, IL: National Council of Teachers of English.

Acknowledgments

First and foremost, I would like to acknowledge the amazing work of my co-author, Dr. Alyce Hunter. As many authors before me have realized, having a second set of life experiences can add dimension and style to a manuscript that a single author cannot. It can also be a necessity when the scope of the work exceeds expectations! In this case, Alyce's addition to the project was critical to its completion. Alyce not only enthusiastically joined me on this project, she did so with style, grace, creativity, pedagogical expertise, and above all, speed and diligence to detail. This book would not be possible without her experience, writing talent, and positive participation, and I am indeed very thankful she was willing to join me on this journey.

I'd like to also thank colleagues along the way for all that they have done to support my expanding knowledge of social studies instruction. Conchi was always willing to simply pass along her most successful activities without expecting anything in return, no matter how long it had taken her to develop them. Julie helped us discover that technology can connect with social studies in many more ways than a reenactment of travels along the Oregon Trail. In addition, I owe Elizabeth special thanks for the opportunity to work with her students with disabilities to discover what modifications could make the activities more universally accessible.

My friends and colleagues at "The Museum" were invaluable in helping me to better understand social science as an area of research and the many ways researchers explore our past and present. All taught me the importance of data collection and evidence and tutored me in appropriate methods of cultural interpretation. They provided patient explanations of objects in the collections and engaged with me in discussions on educational techniques. And although we may hold differing opinions to this day, that is, after all, an element of the inquiry process, and I am forever indebted to their willingness to share their passion for history and culture.

My former university students furthered my experience in working with culturally and linguistically diverse audiences as well as provided me with feedback on which strategies they found especially helpful and those which were better left in the filing cabinet. Phyllis and Charlie are owed great thanks for lending me priceless antiques at a moment's notice and asking not a single question about what exactly I was going to do with them. Kimberly, thank you for being willing to tackle it all, from social studies inquiry kits to providing me with titles of culturally relevant literature under the tightest of deadlines. You are an author, professor, and colleague I very much admire.

I owe much thanks to the long-time support of Amy and Linda—from whom I learned to always say yes to opportunity, and figure out the logistics later. My sincerest thanks also to Allyson for her continued support of all my writing endeavors.

As this goes to press, I am currently seated in my new position at the Lincoln Park Zoo. You might think as I once did that my position at the zoo might place my work in social studies on permanent hiatus. I then discovered our holdings of nearly 150 years of archives chronicling every aspect of life at the zoo. Photos, documents, newspaper clippings, diaries, and ledgers, priceless archives that remind us history is indeed everywhere we look. And as some might suggest . . . enough material for the next book project. . . .

—Leah Melber

I would like to acknowledge my gratitude to Dr. Leah Melber, the inspiration, motivation, and intelligence behind this book and my contribution to it. I feel most blessed to have been asked by Leah to work on such an important publication. I truly admire her desire to provide teachers with practical and usable strategies to assist them with the integration of language arts and social studies. Her zeal, professionalism, and inquiring spirit have guided my ideas, my words, my writing. Thank you, Leah.

I would also like to express my appreciation to my husband, Bob. For almost 40 years, he has provided advice and support. I am particularly grateful for the confidence he has shown in me and our remarkable sons, daughters, sons-in-law, daughters-in-law, grandsons, and granddaughters.

—Alyce Hunter

We also thank the reviewers who provided feedback on the idea for the book and drafts of the strategies:

Lewis Asimeng Boahene, Pennsylvania State University

Karen Enos, Chadron State College

Barbara M. Hanes, Widener University

Ruth A. Johnston, Valparaiso University

Beth A. Moore, Franklin College

JungDuk (JD) Ohn, James Madison University

Kelley Samblis, University of Southern Mississippi

IRA/NCTE Standards for the English Language Arts

The vision guiding these standards is that all students must have the opportunities and resources to develop the language skills they need to pursue life's goals and to participate fully as informed, productive members of society. These standards assume that literacy growth begins before children enter school as they experience and experiment with literacy activities—reading and writing, and associating spoken words with their graphic representations. Recognizing this fact, these standards encourage the development of curriculum and instruction that make productive use of the emerging literacy abilities that children bring to school. Furthermore, the standards provide ample room for the innovation and creativity essential to teaching and learning. They are not prescriptions for particular curriculum or instruction. Although we present these standards as a list, we want to emphasize that they are not distinct and separable; they are, in fact, interrelated and should be considered as a whole.

1. Students read a wide range of print and nonprint texts to build an understanding of texts, of themselves, and of the cultures of the United States and the world; to acquire new information; to respond to the needs and demands of society and the workplace; and for personal fulfillment. Among these texts are fiction and nonfiction, classic and contemporary works.

2. Students read a wide range of literature from many periods in many genres to build an understanding of the many dimensions (e.g., philosophical, ethical, aesthetic) of human experience.

3. Students apply a wide range of strategies to comprehend, interpret, evaluate, and appreciate texts. They draw on their prior experience, their interactions with other readers and writers, their knowledge of word meaning and of other texts, their word identification strategies, and their understanding of textual features (e.g., sound–letter correspondence, sentence structure, context, graphics).

4. Students adjust their use of spoken, written, and visual language (e.g., conventions, style, vocabulary) to communicate effectively with a variety of audiences and for different purposes.

5. Students employ a wide range of strategies as they write and use different writing process elements appropriately to communicate with different audiences for a variety of purposes.

6. Students apply knowledge of language structure, language conventions (e.g., spelling and punctuation), media techniques, figurative language, and genre to create, critique, and discuss print and nonprint texts.

7. Students conduct research on issues and interests by generating ideas and questions, and by posing problems. They gather, evaluate, and synthesize data from a variety of sources (e.g., print and nonprint texts, artifacts, people) to communicate their discoveries in ways that suit their purpose and audience.

8. Students use a variety of technological and informational resources (e.g., libraries, databases, computer networks, video) to gather and synthesize information and to create and communicate knowledge.

9. Students develop an understanding of and respect for diversity in language use, patterns, and dialects across cultures, ethnic groups, geographic regions, and social roles.

10. Students whose first language is not English make use of their first language to develop competency in the English language arts and to develop understanding of content across the curriculum.

11. Students participate as knowledgeable, reflective, creative, and critical members of a variety of literacy communities.

12. Students use spoken, written, and visual language to accomplish their own purposes (e.g., for learning, enjoyment, persuasion, and the exchange of information).

Source: Page3/excerpts from International Reading Association & National Council of Teachers of English. (1996). *Standards for the English Language Arts.* Copyright 1996 by the International Reading Association & National Council of Teachers of English.

NCSS Curriculum Standards for Social Studies

I. CULTURE

Social studies programs should include experiences that provide for the study of culture and cultural diversity.

Human beings create, learn, and adapt culture. Culture helps us to understand ourselves as both individuals and members of various groups. Human cultures exhibit both similarities and differences. We all, for example, have systems of beliefs, knowledge, values, and traditions. Each system also is unique. In a democratic and multicultural society, students need to understand multiple perspectives that derive from different cultural vantage points. This understanding will allow them to relate to people in our nation and throughout the world.

Cultures are dynamic and ever-changing. The study of culture prepares students to ask and answer questions such as: What are the common characteristics of different cultures? How do belief systems, such as religion or political ideals of the culture, influence the other parts of the culture? How does the culture change to accommodate different ideas and beliefs? What does language tell us about the culture? In schools, this theme typically appears in units and courses dealing with geography, history, and anthropology, as well as multicultural topics across the curriculum.

During the early years of school, the exploration of the concepts of likenesses and differences in school subjects such as language arts, mathematics, science, music, and art makes the study of culture appropriate. Socially, the young learner is beginning to interact with other students, some of whom are like the student and some different; naturally, he or she wants to know more about others. In the middle grades, students begin to explore and ask questions about the nature of culture and specific aspects of culture, such as language and beliefs, and the influence of those aspects on human behavior. As students progress through high school, they can understand and use complex cultural concepts such as adaptation, assimilation, acculturation, diffusion, and dissonance drawn from anthropology, sociology, and other disciplines to explain how culture and cultural systems function.

II. TIME, CONTINUITY, & CHANGE

Social studies programs should include experiences that provide for the study of the ways human beings view themselves in and over time.

Human beings seek to understand their historical roots and to locate themselves in time. Such understanding involves knowing what things were like in the past and how things change and develop. Knowing how to read and reconstruct the past allows one to develop a historical perspective and to answer questions such as: Who am I? What happened in the past? How am I connected to those in the past? How has the world changed and how might it change in the future? Why does our personal sense of relatedness to the past change? How can the perspective we have about our own life experiences be viewed as part of the larger human story across time? How do our personal stories reflect varying points of view and inform contemporary ideas and actions?

This theme typically appears in courses that: 1) include perspectives from various aspects of history; 2) draw upon historical knowledge during the examination of social issues; and 3) develop the habits of mind that historians and scholars in the humanities and social sciences employ to study the past and its relationship to the present in the United States and other societies.

Learners in early grades gain experience with sequencing to establish a sense of order and time. They enjoy hearing stories of the recent past as well as of long ago. In addition, they begin to recognize that individuals may hold different views about the past and to understand the linkages between human decisions and consequences. Thus, the foundation is laid for the development of historical knowledge, skills, and values. In the middle grades, students, through a more formal study of history, continue to expand their understanding of the past and of historical concepts and inquiry. They begin to understand and appreciate differences in historical perspectives, recognizing that interpretations are influenced by individual experiences, societal values, and cultural traditions. High school students engage in more sophisticated analysis and reconstruction of the past, examining its relationship to the present and extrapolating into the future. They integrate individual stories about people, events, and situations to form a more holistic conception, in which continuity and change are linked in time and across cultures. Students also learn to draw on their knowledge of history to make informed choices and decisions in the present.

III. People, Places, & Environments

Social studies programs should include experiences that provide for the study of people, places, and environments.

Technological advances connect students at all levels to the world beyond their personal locations. The study of people, places, and human-environment interactions assists learners as they create their spatial views and geographic perspectives of the world. Today's social, cultural, economic, and civic demands on individuals mean that students will need the knowledge, skills, and understanding to ask and answer questions such as: Where are things located? Why are they located where they are? What patterns are reflected in the groupings of things? What do we mean by region? How do landforms change? What implications do these changes have for people? This area of study helps learners make informed and critical decisions about the relationship between human beings and their environment. In schools, this theme typically appears in units and courses dealing with area studies and geography.

In the early grades, young learners draw upon immediate personal experiences as a basis for exploring geographic concepts and skills. They also express interest in things distant and unfamiliar and have concern for the use and abuse of the physical environment. During the middle school years, students relate their personal experiences to happenings in other environmental contexts. Appropriate experiences will encourage increasingly abstract thought as students use data and apply skills in analyzing human behavior in relation to its physical and cultural environment. Students in high school are able to apply geographic understanding across a broad range of fields, including the fine arts, sciences, and humanities. Geographic concepts become central to learners' comprehension of global connections as they expand their knowledge of diverse cultures, both historical and contemporary. The importance of core geographic themes to public policy is recognized and should be explored as students address issues of domestic and international significance.

IV. Individual Development & Identity

Social studies programs should include experiences that provide for the study of individual development and identity.

Personal identity is shaped by one's culture, by groups, and by institutional influences. How do people learn? Why do people behave as they do? What influences how people learn, perceive, and grow? How do people meet their basic needs in a variety of contexts? Questions such as these are central to the study of how individuals develop from youth to adulthood. Examination of various forms of human behavior enhances understanding of the relationships among social norms and emerging personal identities, the social processes that influence identity formation, and the ethical principles underlying individual action. In schools, this theme typically appears in units and courses dealing with psychology and anthropology.

Given the nature of individual development and our own cultural context, students need to be aware of the processes of learning, growth, and development at every level of their school experience. In the early grades, for example, observing brothers, sisters, and older adults, looking at family photo albums, remembering past achievements and projecting oneself into the future, and comparing the patterns of behavior evident in people of different age groups are appropriate activities because young learners develop their personal identities in the context of families, peers, schools, and communities. Central to this development are the exploration, identification, and analysis of how individuals relate to others. In the middle grades, issues of personal identity are refocused as the individual begins to explain self in relation to others in the society and culture. At the high school level, students need to encounter multiple opportunities to examine contemporary patterns of human behavior, using methods from the behavioral sciences to apply core concepts drawn from psychology, social psychology, sociology, and anthropology as they apply to individuals, societies, and cultures.

V. Individuals, Groups, & Institutions

Social studies programs should include experiences that provide for the study of interactions among individuals, groups, and institutions.

Institutions such as schools, churches, families, government agencies, and the courts all play an integral role in our lives. These and other institutions exert enormous influence over us, yet institutions are no more than organizational embodiments to further the core social values of those who comprise them. Thus, it is important that students know how institutions are formed, what controls and influences them, how they control and influence individuals and culture, and how institutions can be maintained or changed. The study of individuals, groups, and institutions, drawing upon sociology, anthropology, and other disciplines, prepares students to ask and answer questions such as: What is the role of institutions in this and other societies? How am I influenced by institutions? How do institutions change? What is my role in institutional change? In schools, this theme typically appears in units and courses dealing with sociology, anthropology, psychology, political science, and history.

Young children should be given opportunities to examine various institutions that affect their lives and influence their thinking. They should be assisted in recognizing the tensions that occur when the goals, values, and principles of two or more institutions or groups conflict-for example, when the school board prohibits candy machines in schools vs. a class project to install a candy machine to help raise money for the local hospital. They should also have opportunities to explore ways in which institutions such as churches or health care networks are created to respond to changing individual and group needs. Middle school learners will benefit from varied experiences through which they examine the ways in which institutions change over time, promote social conformity, and influence culture. They should be encouraged to use this understanding to suggest ways to work through institutional change for the common good. High school students must understand the paradigms and traditions that undergird social and political institutions. They should be provided opportunities to examine, use, and add to the body of knowledge related to the behavioral sciences and social theory as it relates to the ways people and groups organize themselves around common needs, beliefs, and interests.

VI. POWER, AUTHORITY, & GOVERNANCE

Social studies programs should include experiences that provide for the study of how people create and change structures of power, authority, and governance.

Understanding the historical development of structures of power, authority, and governance and their evolving functions in contemporary U.S. society, as well as in other parts of the world, is essential for developing civic competence. In exploring this theme, students confront questions such as: What is power? What forms does it take? Who holds it? How is it gained, used, and justified? What is legitimate authority? How are governments created, structured, maintained, and changed? How can we keep government responsive to its citizens' needs and interests? How can individual rights be protected within the context of majority rule? By examining the purposes and characteristics of various governance systems, learners develop an understanding of how groups and nations attempt to resolve conflicts and seek to establish order and security. Through study of the dynamic relationships among individual rights and responsibilities, the needs of social groups, and concepts of a just society, learners become more effective problem-solvers and decision-makers when addressing the persistent issues and social problems encountered in public life. They do so by applying concepts and methods of political science and law. In schools, this theme typically appears in units and courses dealing with government, politics, political science, history, law, and other social sciences.

Learners in the early grades explore their natural and developing sense of fairness and order as they experience relationships with others. They develop an increasingly comprehensive awareness of rights and responsibilities in specific contexts. During the middle school years, these rights and responsibilities are applied in more complex contexts with emphasis on new applications. High school students develop their abilities in the use of abstract principles. They study the various systems that have been developed over the centuries to allocate and employ power and authority in the governing process. At every level, learners should have opportunities to apply their knowledge and skills to and participate in the workings of the various levels of power, authority, and governance.

VII. PRODUCTION, DISTRIBUTION, & CONSUMPTION

Social studies programs should include experiences that provide for the study of how people organize for the production, distribution, and consumption of goods and services.

People have wants that often exceed the limited resources available to them. As a result, a variety of ways have been invented to decide upon answers to four fundamental questions: What is to be produced? How is production to be organized? How are goods and services to be distributed? What is the most effective allocation of the factors of production (land, labor, capital, and management)? Unequal distribution of resources necessitates systems of exchange, including trade, to improve the well-being of the economy, while the role of government in economic policymaking varies over time and from place to place. Increasingly these decisions are global in scope and require systematic study of an interdependent world economy and the role of technology in economic decision-making. In schools, this theme typically appears in units and courses dealing with concepts, principles, and issues drawn from the discipline of economics.

Young learners begin by differentiating between wants and needs. They explore economic decisions as they compare their own economic experiences with those of others and consider the wider consequences of those decisions on groups, communities, the nation, and beyond. In the middle grades, learners expand their knowledge of economic concepts and principles, and use economic reasoning processes in addressing issues related to the four fundamental economic questions. High school students develop economic perspectives and deeper understanding of key economic concepts and processes through systematic study of a range of economic and sociopolitical systems, with particular emphasis on the examination of domestic and global economic policy options related to matters such as health care, resource use, unemployment, and trade.

VIII. Science, Technology, & Society

Social studies programs should include experiences that provide for the study of relationships among science, technology, and society.

Technology is as old as the first crude tool invented by prehistoric humans, but today's technology forms the basis for some of our most difficult social choices. Modern life as we know it would be impossible without technology and the science that supports it. But technology brings with it many questions: Is new technology always better than that which it will replace? What can we learn from the past about how new technologies result in broader social change, some of which is unanticipated? How can we cope with the ever-increasing pace of change, perhaps even with the feeling that technology has gotten out of control? How can we manage technology so that the greatest number of people benefit from it? How can we preserve our fundamental values and beliefs in a world that is rapidly becoming one technology-linked village? This theme appears in units or courses dealing with history, geography, economics, and civics and government. It draws upon several scholarly fields from the natural and physical sciences, social sciences, and the humanities for specific examples of issues and the knowledge base for considering responses to the societal issues related to science and technology.

Young children can learn how technologies form systems and how their daily lives are intertwined with a host of technologies. They can study how basic technologies such as ships, automobiles, and airplanes have evolved and how we have employed technology such as air conditioning, dams, and irrigation to modify our physical environment. From history (their own and others'), they can construct examples of how technologies such as the wheel, the stirrup, and the transistor radio altered the course of history. By the middle grades, students can begin to explore the complex relationships among technology, human values, and behavior. They will find that science and technology bring changes that surprise us and even challenge our beliefs, as in the case of discoveries and their applications related to our universe, the genetic basis of life, atomic physics, and others. As they move from the middle grades to high school, students will need to think more deeply about how we can manage technology so that we control it rather than the other way around. There should be opportunities to confront such issues as the consequences of using robots to produce goods, the protection of privacy in the age of computers and electronic surveillance, and the opportunities and challenges of genetic engineering, test-tube life, and medical technology with all their implications for longevity and quality of life and religious beliefs.

IX. Global Connections

Social studies programs should include experiences that provide for the study of global connections and interdependence.

The realities of global interdependence require understanding the increasingly important and diverse global connections among world societies. Analysis of tensions between national interests and global priorities contributes to the development of possible solutions to persistent and emerging global issues in many fields: health care, economic development, environmental quality, universal human rights, and others. Analyzing patterns and relationships within and among world cultures, such as economic competition and interdependence, age-old ethnic enmities, political and military alliances, and others, helps learners carefully examine policy alternatives that have both national and global implications. This theme typically appears in units or courses dealing with geography, culture, and economics, but again can draw upon the natural and physical sciences and the humanities, including literature, the arts, and language.

Through exposure to various media and first-hand experiences, young learners become aware of and are affected by events on a global scale. Within this context, students in early grades examine and explore global connections and basic issues and concerns, suggesting and initiating responsive action plans. In the middle years, learners can initiate analysis of the interactions among states and nations and their cultural complexities as they respond to global events and changes. At the high school level, students are able to think systematically about personal, national, and global decisions, interactions, and consequences, including addressing critical issues such as peace, human rights, trade, and global ecology.

X. Civic Ideals & Practices

Social studies programs should include experiences that provide for the study of the ideals, principles, and practices of citizenship in a democratic republic.

An understanding of civic ideals and practices of citizenship is critical to full participation in society and is a central purpose of the social studies. All people have a stake in examining civic ideals and practices across time and in diverse societies as well as at home, and in determining how to close the gap between present practices and the ideals upon which our democratic republic is based. Learners confront such questions as: What is civic participation and how can I be involved? How has the meaning of citizenship evolved? What is the balance between rights and responsibilities? What is the role of the citizen in the community and the nation, and as a member of the world community? How can I make a positive difference? In schools, this theme typically appears in units or courses dealing with history, political science, cultural anthropology, and fields such as global studies and law-related education, while also drawing upon content from the humanities.

In the early grades, students are introduced to civic ideals and practices through activities such as helping to set classroom expectations, examining experiences in relation to ideals, and determining how to balance the needs of individuals and the group. During these years, children also experience views of citizenship in other times and places through stories and drama. By the middle grades, students expand their ability to analyze and evaluate the relationships between ideals and practice. They are able to see themselves taking civic roles in their communities. High school students increasingly recognize the rights and responsibilities of citizens in identifying societal needs, setting directions for public policies, and working to support both individual dignity and the common good. They learn by experience how to participate in community service and political activities and how to use democratic process to influence public policy.

Source: National Council for the Social Studies, *Expectations of excellence: Curriculum standards for social studies* (Washington, DC: NCSS, 1994). This book may be purchased by calling 800–683–0812. Electronic copies of it are not available.

UNIT I
Building Research Skills

———————————————————————————◆

The National Council for the Social Studies' (NCSS; 1994) curriculum standards emphasize the importance of providing students with opportunities to model the processes and research methods of social science researchers such as archaeologists, historians, and anthropologists. Following an inquiry-based model of social studies, students will be involved in investigations in which they pose questions of personal interest and use data to form their own explanations and interpretations of historical events and information (Steeves, 2005).

Developing research skills on the part of students in the area of social studies naturally ties to authentic integration of language arts. Social scientists are constantly reading documents, building their comprehension of a particular event or topic. Publishing results of their work in articles and books is a critical part of a social scientist's job. Oral communication skills are equally important to social scientists as they rely on communicating with colleagues and presenting their findings at annual meetings to both share their discoveries and move toward new ones. When students take part in activities that parallel these authentic uses of language arts, not only do they gain a more accurate understanding of the work of social scientists, but they are provided with the opportunity to use language arts themselves in an authentic context.

As part of the research process, the use of primary sources is critical to the work of the social scientist. Thus, providing students with access to primary sources is a crucial component of an inquiry-based social studies program (Chapin, 2005). Primary sources include documents written by individuals who were part of a historic time or event. However, they also include artifacts, photographs, films, and other items (Chapin, 2005). Providing students with the opportunity to apply critical-thinking skills to exploration of these sources and the complex issues that make up our social studies curriculum is crucial to the development of thoughtful individuals who are well poised to be active citizens in their community and beyond (Shiveley, 2004).

In this unit, instructional techniques are highlighted that will help build students' inquiry skills, providing the opportunity to use primary sources and explore key concepts in the social studies, all strongly integrated with language arts.

REFERENCES

Chapin, J. R. (2005). *Elementary social studies: A practical guide.* Boston: Allyn & Bacon.

National Council for the Social Studies. (1994). *Expectations of excellence: Curriculum standards for social studies.* Washington, DC: Author.

Shiveley, J. M. (2004). Critical thinking and visiting websites: It must be elementary. *Social Studies and the Young Learner, 16*(4), 9–12.

Steeves, K. A. (2005). History: Uncovering the past through inquiry. In R. H. Audet & L. K. Jordan (Eds.), *Integrating inquiry across the curriculum* (pp. 65–84). Thousand Oaks, CA: Corwin Press.

Teaching Observation, Questioning, and Inference

Strategy 1

MYSTERY ARTIFACT INVESTIGATION

Sarah squinted at her mystery object, a round glass ball about the size of a large orange. Living her whole life in Utah, she had no idea that this was a replica of an antique fishing float used to keep nets from sinking to the bottom of the ocean. Before beginning to write, she looked over at her neighbor but quickly realized James had been assigned a different object. He would not be of any help to her. Her partner Keisha asked her why she was frowning. Sarah answered with a sigh, "I just wish I knew if this is something that would be used as decoration or to actually *do* something."

Keisha smiled, "Hey, that's a part of the assignment. Look, it asks what kinds of questions you have!" Sarah quickly turned her frown into a smile and began to add her question to the correct part of the data sheet. Who would have thought having questions without answers was still doing social studies?!

Many students feel doing social studies means having someone else tell them the answers. But reading about a historic figure in a textbook or memorizing the capitals of each state could not be further from the work of practicing social scientists. In fact, current research in the area of social studies posits that "real learning is founded on questions, not answers" (Harada & Kim, 2003, p. 33). By creating opportunities for students to carefully observe, make inferences, and share their discoveries, they are given the opportunity to build problem-solving skills that are advocated by social studies national standards (NCSS, 1994) and that are helpful across all academic areas.

One way to develop critical-thinking skills on the part of students is by encouraging them to carefully deconstruct the details of an everyday object or artifact. By selecting something that may be unfamiliar to students, this instructional technique can further tap into students' problem-solving skills. Data sheets have been proven to help guide student responses and focus explorations. However, open-ended data sheets have proven to be most effective in this area (Mortensen & Smart, 2007). This open-ended format allows for emphasis to be placed on observing details and planning for further information gathering rather than blind guesses as to an artifact's identity or purpose.

Anything can be used as a mystery artifact. Artifacts are defined as "any object made by human beings" (Dictionary.com Unabridged, n.d.) so the options are broad. Sources for artifacts include garage sales or swap meets as well as the homes or garages of family or relatives (Melber, 2008). What is important to remember is that students 12 and younger may find something that is commonplace to you (i.e., an 8-track cassette!) is novel or unique to them. With an emphasis on firsthand experience and exposure, artifact selection should be guided by students' developmental level, resulting in artifacts that are not fragile, are able to be handled enthusiastically, and will spark communication and discussion among young investigators in line with a constructivist approach.

Please visit www.sagepub.com/lmelberstudy for the updated National Council of the Social Studies standards.

Curriculum Standards for Social Studies

- Strand I: Culture
- Strand II: Time, Continuity, & Change
- Strand III: People, Places, & Environments
- Strand IV: Individual Development & Identity

Standards for the English Language Arts

Students will develop expository writing skills through the completion of the data sheet. Sharing their discoveries with their peers supports oral language skills.

- Standard 5:   Students employ a wide range of strategies as they write and use different writing process elements appropriately to communicate with different audiences for a variety of purposes.

Technology Connection

Students can use the Internet to search for information about their artifact. The open-ended data sheet focuses students to the extent that they know what to search for and how to narrow down extensive results. The "image search" function on many search engines, using the key words students have identified on their data sheets, can also be helpful to their research.

Sources: National Council for the Social Studies, 1994; National Council of Teachers of English and International Reading Association, 1996.

KEY THEMES

Making careful observations

Analyzing observational data

Identifying areas for future study

MATERIALS

Data sheets (provided)

Pencils/pens

Colored pencils/crayons

Enough objects for every two students (for a list of suggested objects, see box below)

Object/Artifact Suggestions

multicultural textiles

bundled sage

glass fishing float

incense cone

packet of spice

wood carving

antique railroad tie

foreign coin/currency

odd cooking utensil (cherry pitter, egg slicer, etc.)

PROCEDURES

Begin the instruction by discussing the work of social scientists with students as a whole class. Images from the Internet, children's books, and even excerpts from educational television can provide excellent firsthand exposure to the work of a historian, anthropologist, or archaeologist (see Web site examples in Strategy 4). Explain to students that all social scientists are good researchers. Among what makes them good researchers is that they can make careful observations, they know how to find out important information, and they are able to take all that they discover and draw a conclusion or form an opinion. This activity will allow students to replicate the work of social scientists and develop their own research skills.

For the second part of the instruction, place students in pairs. With this instructional model, groups with more than two can sometimes result in some students taking too passive of a role in the investigation. It also limits the hands-on time each student can be allotted due to logistical reasons. Provide each student pair with an object and two data sheets (see Figure 1.1 on p. 8). Although students are encouraged to explore together and discuss their thoughts with their partner, they will have their own data sheet to record their discoveries. Social scientists do not always agree!

Before students begin to work independently, scaffolding use of the data sheet will be critical. Many students like to simply list "Internet" as the place they will go for more information. Emphasize the importance of more information here, such as what search terms will be used or what type of Web page would be most helpful. Another common response is "library." If that is the case, what type of book will students want to review? This activity focuses just on the planning of investigations, so unless it is conducted as an extension, students will not be searching the Internet unsupervised. Rather, it is to develop planning skills and support students in thinking critically about the best places to go for more information.

Provide ample time for students to investigate their artifact and record their discoveries on their data sheets. Monitoring as students complete the activity will prove helpful, as some students will need more scaffolding to complete the data sheet than others. After years of emphasis on identifying one right answer, some students need support in adjusting to this technique focused on the process of investigation rather than simply the outcome. It will also be important to clarify the length of response that is expected. This will vary by grade level.

After students have completed their data sheets, regroup students into teams of four. This is an opportunity for students to "report out" their discoveries and preliminary conclusions to their peers. This is a time where they may be able to benefit from any knowledge their peers might have. Depending on the artifacts that have been chosen for investigation, strategically placing pairs with similar items together can support the investigation process and lead to even more thoughtful conclusions.

At the end of the activity, data sheets can be collected and scored. Many students will be curious about the artifacts of their peers. Providing time for circulating among groups and exploring all the artifacts can be very enjoyable for students. Providing the students with "answers" should be deemphasized. Rather, a group discussion about what the class discovered about the different artifacts should be conducted. Usually, carefully scaffolded group discussion will result in students discovering specific content such as artifact use or identity on their own, without the need for direct instruction on the part of the teacher. Examples include asking students to describe the materials used to create the object, encouraging them to notice details that belie its age, or even drawing comparisons to things they might already have knowledge of. Plans can also be made to provide students with access to the Internet or an expert in order to follow through with their plans for additional information gathering.

This instructional technique can be replicated throughout the school year. Providing students with repeated exposure to observation, questioning, and communicating results will hone these skills as well as build students' confidence in their investigation abilities. Repeated use of the data sheet usually results in more extensive responses and detailed narrative, also supporting language arts development alongside social science inquiry skills.

GRADE-LEVEL MODIFICATIONS

K–2nd Grade

Because of limited writing skills, emphasis on scientific illustration and the inclusion of a word bank will be critical. Also, selection of items that have familiar uses will be important so even when the item is identified, students can have an understanding of its role or importance.

3rd Grade–5th Grade

Students at this level will most likely have a great deal of opinions and ideas but may not capture their thoughts in written format with adequate detail. Provide specific length guidelines and, if necessary, provide an example as guidance. Students at this grade level will be better able to think abstractly and can learn from objects that may have uses they are not familiar with.

6th Grade–8th Grade

Students at this grade level enjoy being successful and are proud of the knowledge that they have. It may prove difficult to "stump" them, so the emphasis should instead be on identifying truly key questions they would like answered to know more as well as being very specific as to where further information about the object can be located. Novelty will be well-received with this grade level.

MEETING THE NEEDS OF ENGLISH LEARNERS

The realia at the center of this instructional technique will support English learners by creating a context-rich environment. The partner format of the experience will also be supportive of English learners. Additional support can be provided to English learners by creating a word bank containing vocabulary that students are likely to want to include in their narrative description. Last, the data sheet can be modified to provide less emphasis on narrative description and more emphasis on sketches and diagrams that can be labeled with single words or phrases supported by the provided word bank.

MEETING THE NEEDS OF STUDENTS WITH SPECIAL NEEDS

To support students with physical disabilities, particularly fine motor control, selection of artifacts is a critical consideration. Select items that can be handled easily and that will be durable enough for unintentional rough handling. The reciprocal teaching element of this activity will be especially helpful with reinforcing content for students with learning disabilities. Additional modifications can include modified expectations for length and detail of written component or the opportunity to share discoveries orally.

ASSESSMENT SUGGESTION

At the conclusion of the activity, students will be able to:

- Carefully illustrate a historic object
- Summarize observations in narrative form
- Pose questions for further study
- Identify areas where further data can be collected
- Summarize findings in narrative form

Students' data sheets can be assessed by using a simple rubric such as the following:

Score	Criteria
4	All six sections of the data sheet are completed with exceptional detail and insight.
3	All six sections are completed with an acceptable level of detail.
2	Three to five sections are completed with an acceptable amount of detail, or all sections completed with significant errors.
1	Fewer than three sections are completed, or multiple errors are present.

Children's Literature Connection

The Room of Wonders
   By Sergio Ruzzier
   ISBN: 978–0374363437
   This work follows a young boy as he collects everyday items to feed his curiosity about the world around him.

Quick Fact

When studying an object or artifact, the context in which the item was discovered is critical to a historian. That's why museums record all the details of where an item was discovered, any date that can be attributed to it, as well as any connection it might have to other elements of the historic narrative. A stove from the 1800s without context can tell us about early cooking practices. A stove documented as discovered adjacent to the Oregon Trail along with other "heavy items" tells us much more about the hardships of overland travel and coping strategies of early pioneers.

FIGURE 1.1 Mystery Artifact Sample Data Sheet   3rd–5th, 6th–8th

1. Illustrate your object below.

2. Describe your object below:

_____

_____

3. What questions do you have about your object?

a. _____

_____

b. _____

_____

c. _____

_____

4. Where could you go for more information about your object?

a. _____

_____

b. _____

_____

c. _____

_____

5. How do you think your object might have been used?

_____

_____

6. What other conclusions can you draw about your object?

_____

_____

REFERENCES

Dictionary.com Unabridged (v 1.1). (n.d.). Retrieved May 15, 2009, from http://dictionary .reference.com

Harada, V., & Kim, L. (2003). Problem-based instruction makes learning real. *Knowledge Quest, 32*(1), 33–34.

Melber, L. M. (2008). *Informal learning and field trips: Engaging students in standards based experiences across the K–5 curriculum*. Thousand Oaks, CA: Corwin Press.

Mortensen, M. F., & Smart, K. (2007). Free-choice worksheets increase students' exposure to curriculum during museum visits. *Journal of Research in Science Teaching, 44*, 1389–1414.

National Council for the Social Studies. (1994). *Expectations of excellence: Curriculum standards for social studies*. Washington, DC: Author.

National Council of Teachers of English and International Reading Association. (1996). *Standards for the English language arts*. Urbana, IL: National Council of Teachers of English.

Strategy 2

Oral Histories in the Curriculum

CONDUCTING INTERVIEWS

Juan's grandmother smiled as he sat her down in her favorite chair and sat across from her with a notepad and pencil. She always enjoyed time with her grandson, but was surprised that she could actually help him with his homework. She hadn't lived in this country for very long and didn't speak English very well. When Juan asked if he could interview her for school, she was afraid that she would not be able to help. It was exciting for her to learn she could speak to her grandson in Spanish. Not only was it fun to tell him about her life in Mexico, it felt good to know that listening in Spanish and then completing his homework in English would help him become a better student. He explained that the assignment would help him with his listening and writing, as well as help him understand things that children liked long ago. Understanding the past was actually part of his school curriculum!

Once they were comfortable, Juan asked his grandmother to start by telling him about her favorite foods when she was his age. This was an easy question for his grandmother. It is the same thing she makes for him around Christmas time: Tamales!

Oral histories provide social scientists with exceptionally rich data about lifeways of the past and experiences of diverse populations. Recordings and transcripts of oral histories are examples of primary sources used by social scientists and thus should be included in the elementary social studies curriculum as well.

Oral histories are powerful sources of information for many reasons. First, they often document the stories of marginalized or immigrant populations who may not have left traditional records of their life experiences (Olmedo, 1996). In addition, the "first-voice" nature of an oral history provides a forum for a true diversity of experience, thoughts, and opinions (Chapin, 2005). Furthermore, when used in a classroom setting, they provide authentic opportunities to richly integrate with language arts development (Putnam & Rommel-Esham, 2004). Interviews are an excellent way for students to develop historical thinking skills, particularly skills of analysis and interpretation (Nash, Crabtree, & National History Task Force, 1996).

Incorporation of interviews and oral histories in the classroom is an excellent way to bring relevance and life to the classroom social studies curriculum. Collecting oral histories from friends or family members can help students further their understanding of cultural universals, which can provide personal relevance to social studies topics (Alleman, Knighton, & Brophy, 2007). They also promote positive relationships with the community and across generations (Kazemek, Wellik, & Zimmerman, 2002) in line with overarching social studies curriculum goals of supporting students in becoming active, helpful citizens.

Sources: National Council for the Social Studies, 1994; National Council of Teachers of English and International Reading Association, 1996.

Please visit www.sagepub.com/lmelberstudy for the updated National Council of the Social Studies standards.

Curriculum Standards for Social Studies

- Strand I: Culture
- Strand II: Time, Continuity, & Change
- Strand IV: Individual Development & Identify

Standards for the English Language Arts

Oral interviews support students in comprehension of the spoken word as well as effective methods of orally communicating themselves. Allowing students to use their first language during the project is further supportive of language arts development.

- Standard 4:   Students adjust their use of spoken, written, and visual language (e.g., conventions, style, vocabulary) to communicate effectively with a variety of audiences and for different purposes.

- Standard 10: Students whose first language is not English make use of their first language to develop competency in the English language arts and to develop understanding of content across the curriculum.

Technology Connection

Students can incorporate technology to create a multimedia product summarizing the results of their oral interviews. With adequate permission, interviews can be captured using digital video cameras. Students might then create a Web site or PowerPoint presentation to creatively disseminate their discoveries.

Helpful Web site: National Public Radio, "This I Believe" Series, www.thisibelieve.org

This site provides numerous oral histories from individuals on a variety of topics from living through the Vietnam War to fighting world hunger. Not all featured stories will be appropriate for all grade levels so a preview is critical. However, these short features will provide students with the opportunity to hear first-voice accounts of critical issues and events.

KEY THEMES

Gathering qualitative data through interviews

Summarizing qualitative data

Communicating findings and discoveries

MATERIALS

Data sheets (provided)

Pencils/pens

Poster boards

Magazines for collage work

PROCEDURES

Begin the project by explaining to students that many social scientists use interviews to help gather information about how life was many years ago. These interviews can take the form of an oral history, defined as when someone who is alive spends time thinking about and explaining details of their past. Inform students that they will be taking part in an oral history project of their own.

Students will need a specific focus to guide their oral history project. The age of the student will be the most critical factor in determining the best topic for the project (refer to the following specific grade-level guidelines). Whatever the guiding topics are, providing students with a data sheet listing the topics and with space to record key words or phrases will help with the logistics of the activity. Word banks on the data sheets may also prove helpful.

Many students will have different comfort levels with speaking to adults. This may be due to cultural upbringing or simply individual personality traits. To prepare students for the experience, conduct role plays of the interview process. Review how to politely ask a question. Discuss the importance of letting the individual guide the history, even if things seem to go a little off topic. Role play how to respectfully end the experience as well. These role-play activities can be done with peers as well as with the teacher as a whole-class demonstration.

Once students are prepared to gather an oral history, provide them with sufficient time to connect to a friend, neighbor, or family member. A note home explaining the project is imperative so families know how to best support their child (see Figure 2.1 on p. 14). Be sure to let students know the oral histories can be shared in English or in the child's first language. Whatever they and their interviewee are most comfortable with is fine.

The final part of the project will be for students to create a poster outlining what they learned. They will want to include the first name of the person who shared the oral history as well as his or her relationship to the child. The poster should also highlight key points from the oral history, presented in a colorful and creative way, and include photographs, images from the Internet, or pictures from magazines. Specific poster expectations will vary based on student grade level. Students can present their poster to the rest of the class and a follow-up discussion can be held to identify any similarities between information gathered by each student. Posters can be displayed in the classroom or in school hallways.

GRADE-LEVEL MODIFICATIONS

K–2nd Grade

Younger students should focus on topics that will be personally relevant to them. By focusing on how lifestyles of the past might have been both similar and different from their own, this can be accomplished. Examples might include favorite meals, pleasure activities, or methods of dress. The final poster will be simple. The narrative portion can be limited to several key phrases that an adult can assist with. Images from magazines or the Internet can support the narrative message.

3rd Grade–5th Grade

At this grade level, topics can be either personal or connect to key historical events. Poster expectations will be higher at this grade level and include specific narrative expectations. A good number of focus areas is five, with two to three sentences related to each focus area expected on the poster. There will be more narrative than imagery, yet students may arrange the poster in whatever way they choose.

6th Grade–8th Grade

At this grade level, students may want to explore conducting two interviews with individuals who may have different experiences or opinions to reinforce oral interviews as a method of capturing multiple voices. Poster expectations should be more in line with those used by researchers at professional conferences. For example, a tri-fold poster can contain the central question in the center and highlight the "subjects" of the research, the findings, and future areas for study on the flanking sides. Images should be directly related to the narrative, such as images of focus events or photos of interviewees if given permission. Direct quotes should be included.

MEETING THE NEEDS OF ENGLISH LEARNERS

Sometimes the oral fluency of English learners may be more developed than written fluency. The opportunity to rely on conversational English, with limited academic vocabulary, will in itself be an element of this instructional strategy that will support the English learners. If further modification is needed, allowing students to conduct their interview in the language of their choice can make the activity more accessible for their fluency level. This is in line with national standards of language arts. Another option is to allow students to conduct the oral history with another member of the class and work together on the final project.

MEETING THE NEEDS OF STUDENTS WITH SPECIAL NEEDS

The emphasis on oral communication will be helpful in building the social skills of students with disabilities. Students with learning disabilities may find the oral language emphasis over written work to be an especially good match for their interests and abilities. Work with a students' special-education teacher to identify comfort level with oral interviewing and then permit the student to use a partner if this will increase his or her comfort and performance. Recording devices might be helpful for students with learning disabilities in capturing all necessary information. Students with communication challenges might be well served by working from a list of written questions or prompts that the interviewee can read along with the student.

ASSESSMENT SUGGESTION

At the conclusion of the activity, students will be able to:

- Form questions of personal interest
- Gather information through oral interview
- Summarize qualitative data

Students' final presentation boards can be assessed using the following rubric:

Score	Content Criteria	Presentation Criteria
4	Project contains detailed, clear information in all key areas.	Project is very well organized, neatly completed, and demonstrates the highest effort.
3	Project contains information in all key areas although it is limited in details.	Project is of acceptable quality.
2	Project contains information in fewer than assigned areas with acceptable details.	Project lacks neatness and demonstrates a lack of organizational effort.
1	Project contains minimal information.	Project demonstrates minimal effort.

Children's Literature Connection

African American Voices

By Deborah Gillan Straub

ISBN: 9780810394971

These oral histories help students learn more about the contributions of African Americans throughout history.

FIGURE 2.1   Sample Family Letter: Oral History

Dear Friends and Family Members:

Our class is learning about the past. One way we'd like to find out more about how things were before our third-grade students were born is by conducting an oral history of a friend or family member. The topic we have chosen is: What were the types of things children did for fun when you were young?

   We would love your help! If you'd like to participate, all you have to do is be willing to talk a little about this topic with *insert child's name*. All the rest is up to him or her!

   Thanks so much for your help! This activity will help our students develop their communication skills as well as learn more about the past. Please let me know if you have any questions.

Sincerely,

Mrs. Smith

REFERENCES

Alleman, J., Knighton, B., & Brophy, J. (2007). Social studies: Incorporating all children using community and cultural universals as the centerpiece. *Journal of Learning Disabilities, 40,* 166–173.

Chapin, J. R. (2005). *Elementary social studies: A practical guide.* Boston: Allyn & Bacon.

Kazemek, F., Wellik, J., & Zimmerman, P. (2002). Across the generations. *Journal of Adolescent and Adult Literacy, 45,* 622–624.

Nash, G., Crabtree, E., & National History Task Force. (1996). *National standards for history, basic edition.* Los Angeles: National Center for History in Schools.

National Council for the Social Studies. (1994). *Expectations of excellence: Curriculum standards for social studies.* Washington, DC: Author.

National Council of Teachers of English and International Reading Association. (1996). *Standards for the English language arts.* Urbana, IL: National Council of Teachers of English.

Olmedo, I. M. (1996). Creating contexts for studying history with students learning English. *Social Studies, 87*(1), 39–43.

Putnam, E., & Rommel-Esham, K. (2004). Using oral history to study change: An integrated approach. *The Social Studies, 95*(5), 201–205.

Strategy
3

Data Collection and Analysis

SCHOOL CAR COUNT

"There's another black car!" shouted Jenny.

"Wow, *another* one? We have twice as many black cars as any other color," answered Kim as she made another tally mark on the data sheet.

"Why do we have a category for yellow? I don't see any yellow cars anywhere!" shouted Jenny again from the other side of the parking lot.

"I once saw a yellow car in a magazine—it was some super fast sports car. Maybe only sports cars come in yellow," hypothesized Kyle.

"Yeah, and teachers never drive sports cars!" laughed Kim.

Jenny arrived back at the group panting. "I've got a problem," she said with a frown. "We have two types of blue—dark blue and light blue. Should we keep them in the same category or make a new column?"

Kim looked at Kyle and shrugged. "I think it should be separate but let's call the group together and decide," she answered. "After all, it would definitely be a different color at a car store!"

As researchers, social scientists are consistently collecting and analyzing data. Sometimes these data are qualitative, such as describing the dress of a community or a type of celebration. Other times, the data are quantitative or numeric, such as growth in population over time or distance traveled by a nomadic community over time.

In this chapter, students will be collecting quantitative data to determine the most popular car color in their community. The project is designed as a problem-solving activity in which students are presented with a dilemma. They then not only collect the data but draw conclusions based on the data they collect and analyze. This approach not only supports students in developing research skills, but also in better understanding the true nature and complexity of social science research (McGuire, 2007). The emphasis on finding answers to problems through collaborative group work is aligned with a problem-based learning approach used to promote active thinking on the part of students (Goodnough, 2006).

Research shows that the elementary social studies curriculum does not adequately prepare students for understanding basic economic issues such as goods, services, supply, and demand (Posnanski, Schug, & Schmitt, 2007). With research indicating the important role that everyday objects can play in inquiry-based activities (Alvarado & Herr, 2003), cars were selected as the focus for this activity due to their familiarity to students as well as their availability and the ease of access.

Sources: National Council for the Social Studies, 1994; National Council of Teachers of English and International Reading Association, 1996.

Please visit www.sagepub.com/lmelberstudy for the updated National Council of the Social Studies standards.

Curriculum Standards for Social Studies

- Strand VII: Production, Distribution, & Consumption
- Strand VIII: Science, Technology, & Society

Standards for the English Language Arts

Throughout the data collection phase, students are relying on language arts to communicate with their peers. The final proposal written individually by students is an excellent exercise in persuasive writing, relying on student-collected data as supporting evidence.

- Standard 5:   Students employ a wide range of strategies as they write and use different writing process elements appropriately to communicate with different audiences for a variety of purposes.

- Standard 7:   Students conduct research on issues and interests by generating ideas and questions, and by posing problems. They gather, evaluate, and synthesize data from a variety of sources (e.g., print and nonprint texts, artifacts, people) to communicate their discoveries in ways that suit their purpose and audience.

Technology Connection

Students can use a database program to synthesize their results into charts and graphs. The same program can support students in doing mathematical calculations that may be slightly above their developmental level. Students may also search manufacturers' Web sites to align the data they collected with current trends in the automotive industry.

Helpful Web site: Forbes Autos, www.forbesautos.com

This site provides latest research on popular car colors and models, as well as other information that may prove helpful to students.

KEY THEMES

Collecting and analyzing quantitative data

Exploring economic themes

Applying knowledge to decision making

MATERIALS

Car brochures (These can be procured from a car dealership in small amounts.)

Access to parking lot

Data sheets (provided)

Pens/pencils

Colored pencils/markers

Calculators

PROCEDURES

A great way to start the instruction is by sharing new car brochures with students. Usually these pamphlets have swatches of the different colors available for each model. Students can be placed in groups and provided with one or two pamphlets per group, sharing as necessary. After a few minutes of discussing the color choices in their pamphlets, a short class discussion can be held summarizing their discoveries.

The second part of the discussion can lead into details of goods and services and the basic idea that those who manufacture goods want to market things that the consumer will readily buy. Review that buying a new car is a special purchase and people put much thought into make, model, and color. The students' job will be to pretend they own a car dealership that sells the Super Car 1000. They will be ordering 100 cars for the year to sell and have to decide how many of each color they would like to order. Rather than just guess, they will have to do some market research to help them with their decision.

Arrangements will be made to visit the faculty parking lot (or any other safe area where multiple cars can be observed and counted). They will use the provided data sheets (see Figure 3.1 on p. 21) to record the different colors they see. After recording the data, they will make a graph (see Figure 3.2 on p. 22) summarizing their observations using basic frequency and percentage calculations (calculators can be used as appropriate for grade level). Once they have collected the data and created graphic summaries of their discoveries as a collaborative group, students will be asked to individually write up a final recommendation proposal on how many of each color car they would like to order. The length and language-arts expectations of this can vary from a picture and two to three sentences to a three-page report, depending on the grade level of the students and their linguistic skill base. Students should be encouraged to share their findings with their peers either informally or through whole-class presentation, whichever is most appropriate.

GRADE-LEVEL MODIFICATIONS

K–2nd Grade

In working with younger students, the most appropriate modification of the procedure is to conduct the activity as a whole class, rather than individual groups. This will provide the teacher with the opportunity to scaffold the different aspects of data collection and graphing and model each step as whole-class discussion. Results can be posted on a bulletin board communicating that students are actively involved in data collection and analysis.

3rd Grade–5th Grade

These grade levels will be able to work in their groups with moderate help from the teacher. They will most likely need support with the advanced calculations and should be allowed to use calculators to retain the emphasis on data analysis rather than mathematical computation that may be above their grade-level standards.

6th Grade–8th Grade

At this grade level, students will be able to conduct much of the activity on their own. After conducting the car count on school grounds, with teacher guidance, this grade level can be asked to replicate the activity at home and combine the data for a final report that takes into account several potential "client bases." This grade level may also want to explore issues of customization, popularity of car make and model, or the presence of hybrid automobiles.

MEETING THE NEEDS OF ENGLISH LEARNERS

This activity incorporates a context-embedded approach to understanding economic trends by having students directly analyze a nearby parking lot. This context and use of a cooperative group structure will significantly support English learners and promote individual learning success. In addition, the graphic organizer students will be using to record their data and summarize their results will support English learners in organizing their thoughts and responses. Additional support can be provided by creating a word bank with color names translated into the primary language of the student. Another option is to create an index card with the names of colors listed only in English, but with color swatches next to each new vocabulary word.

MEETING THE NEEDS OF STUDENTS WITH SPECIAL NEEDS

The collaborative nature of the activity will support students with disabilities in participating in the method that is best matched to their abilities. Students with limited gross motor skills will be able to physically navigate a flat, paved area of a parking lot. Each group will have only one data recorder, so students with fine motor impairments might select the job of counting or reporting rather than recording. For students who rely on assistive technology such as an augmentative communication device, it will be helpful to program color names into the device in advance. For students who may have difficulty following directions or impulse control, it will be important to have them assigned to a group with an adult for extra supervision. Depending on student's abilities, assigning them extra responsibility such as ensuring students stay on walkways or taking a regular head count may help keep the student on task and out of harm's way.

ASSESSMENT SUGGESTION

At the conclusion of the activity, students will be able to:

- Collect and analyze numeric data
- Use data to develop a marketing plan
- Communicate decision-making process

This activity has three possible assessment elements: data sheet, graph, and narrative product proposal. These can be assessed using the following rubric:

Score	Data Analysis	Graph	Product Proposal
4	Data sheet is complete, and all calculations are correct.	Graph is complete, and all data are correct.	Proposal accurately and clearly summarizes data from other two sheets to provide a sound recommendation.
3	Data sheet is nearly complete or is mostly correct.	Graph is mostly correct with only small errors or deletions.	Proposal provides clear recommendations with correct data but lacks detail and creativity.
2	Multiple data errors and calculation errors.	Effort is made to complete the graph but there are multiple inaccuracies.	Proposal is incomplete or does not base recommendations on data.
1	Little is correct.	Graph is incomplete or completely inaccurate.	Proposal is not in line with assignment guidelines.

Children's Literature Connection

If I Built a Car
   By Chris Van Dusen
   ISBN: 978–0142408254
DK Eyewitness Books: Cars
   By Richard Sutton and Elizabeth Baquedano
   ISBN: 978–0756613846

From reality to fantasy, these two books provide students with both accurate content information on car design as well as a whimsical plan by a little boy to design the perfect car.

Safety First!

Working around cars, even stationary ones, requires extra safety precautions.

- Check with the school principal to determine if parental permission slips to visit the faculty parking lot are needed. This will vary based on the layout and policy of the individual school.
- Select a time when faculty are unlikely to be coming in and out of the parking lot. There are some lots that actually remain locked during the day, which will ensure cars will not be entering and exiting.
- Send a note to all of the faculty and staff who use the lot alerting them of the project. This will ensure that if they are planning to move their car during your visit, they will be aware students may be nearby and can remain extra vigilant.
- Review safety precautions with children, and point out the safest locations for collecting data, such as on a walkway rather than directly behind a parked car.
- Arrange for parent volunteers to be present that day to work with each group of children. If there is unplanned car movement, every student will be in close proximity to an adult who can actively supervise the situation and intervene when necessary.

Quick Fact

Some car makers comment that when there are downturns or uncertainty in the economy, neutral colors such as silver, white, and black become more popular. Research also indicates that when it comes to resale, neutral colors fare better than brightly colored options.

FIGURE 3.1   Car Color Sample Data Sheet   3rd–5th, 6th–8th

Researcher Names: _____

Date: _____

Field Site Location: _____

Color Tally: Using tally marks, record the number of each color car you see. There are spaces for you to include a color not listed on the chart.

Color	Number	Color	Number
Red	_____	Blue	_____
Green	_____	Yellow	_____
Silver	_____	Maroon	_____
White	_____		
Black	_____		
Gold	_____		

Calculations: Use your calculations to complete the data analysis.

• There were _____ red cars out of _____ total cars. That means _____% of the cars were red.

• There were _____ green cars out of _____ total cars. That means _____% of the cars were green.

• There were _____ silver cars out of _____ total cars. That means _____% of the cars were silver.

• There were _____ white cars out of _____ total cars. That means _____% of the cars were white.

• There were _____ black cars out of _____ total cars. That means _____% of the cars were black.

• There were _____ gold cars out of _____ total cars. That means _____% of the cars were gold.

• There were _____ yellow cars out of _____ total cars. That means _____% of the cars were yellow.

• There were _____ blue cars out of _____ total cars. That means _____% of the cars were blue.

• There were _____ maroon cars out of _____ total cars. That means _____% of the cars were maroon.

The most popular car color was _____ .

The least popular car color was _____ .

| **FIGURE 3.2**   Car Color Sample Graph Sheet | 3rd–5th, 6th–8th |

Researcher Names: _____

Date: _____

Field Site Location: _____

REFERENCES

Alvarado, A. E., & Herr, P. R. (2003). *Inquiry-based learning using everyday objects*. Thousand Oaks, CA: Corwin Press.

Goodnough, K. (2006). Enhancing pedagogical content knowledge through self-study: An exploration of problem-based learning. *Teaching in Higher Education, 11*, 301–318.

McGuire, M. (2007). What happened to social studies? The disappearing curriculum. *Phi Delta Kappan, 88*, 620–624.

National Council for the Social Studies. (1994). *Expectations of excellence: Curriculum standards for social studies*. Washington, DC: Author.

National Council of Teachers of English and International Reading Association. (1996). *Standards for the English language arts*. Urbana, IL: National Council of Teachers of English.

Posnanski, T. J., Schug, M. C., & Schmitt, T. (2007). Can students learn economics and personal finance in specialized elementary school? *International Journal of Social Education, 21*, 196–205.

Using
Authentic Models

Strategy
4

EXPLORING AN ARCHAEOLOGICAL DIG

"I'm only finding all these broken pot pieces! This isn't what a real archaeologist would do at all!" pouted Janice.

"How do you know? Do you know a real archaeologist?" teased Ariana.

"No! But I went to the museum, and none of *those* pots are in pieces," shot back Janice.

Mr. Heyning had been listening in and decided to interject. "Janice, it's true that sometimes archaeologists may find artifacts that are in one piece. A lot of the time however, those artifacts you see in a museum were once in pieces. An archaeologist had to work carefully to locate all the pieces and patiently put them back together."

"Wow," responded Janice. "I guess I *am* doing work like a real archaeologist!"

To provide students with the most authentic social studies experiences, creating authentic models of social science research is critical. An authentic model is one that replicates the process of social science research as accurately as possible. Examples include mock trials, living history experiences, or exploration of artifact replicas.

This chapter uses a model of an archaeological dig to support student understanding. Although archaeological studies are often highly intriguing to students, they also can be areas of study with which students may have difficulty making a personal connection. In this chapter, students will take part in a replication of an archaeological dig. In doing so, they will learn not only the logistics of excavating artifacts and accurately recording data (Weaver & Brown, 2003), but also policy and ethical issues such as ownership and restricted access (Moe, Coleman, Fink, & Krejs, 2002). Archaeological studies specifically offer students the opportunity to actively study history using a method that acknowledges the presence of multiple voices and a plural past (Whitting, 1998). It is a method of actively engaging in the content of our history, through an emphasis on skills and process (Glendinning, 2005).

When students have the opportunity to take part in problem-solving, inquiry-based activities, such as the one profiled in this strategy, they are given the opportunity to control their own learning (Canestrari, 2005). We know that when students are intrinsically motivated and in charge of their own learning, we can often see greater cognitive gains (Covington, 1998). Participation in an archaeological dig provides students with the opportunity to interact with artifacts kinesthetically, use narrative to describe their experiences, and rely on mathematics and art to diagram their discoveries. This mixture of modalities ties well to multiple intelligence theory (Gardner, 1993) and is one method of meeting the learning needs of a diverse student body.

Please visit www.sagepub.com/lmelberstudy for the updated National Council of the Social Studies standards.

Curriculum Standards for Social Studies

- Strand II: Time, Continuity, & Change
- Strand III: People, Places, & Environments
- Strand X: Global Connections

Standards for the English Language Arts

This activity builds written and oral fluency through group participation in the activity, discussion of dilemmas, and completion of the written data sheet.

- Standard 1:   Students read a wide range of print and nonprint texts to build an understanding of texts, of themselves, and of the cultures of the United States and the world; to acquire new information; to respond to the needs and demands of society and the workplace; and for personal fulfillment. Among these texts are fiction and nonfiction, classic and contemporary works.

- Standard 5:   Students employ a wide range of strategies as they write and use different writing process elements appropriately to communicate with different audiences for a variety of purposes.

Technology Connection

Encourage students to review the provided Web sites to better understand the field work of archaeologists as well as the work that occurs in the laboratory or within collections of a museum. In addition, reviewing Web sites that address current issues in the field of archaeology can lead to class discussion and debate.

- US Department of the Interior: Bureau of Land Management, http://www.blm.gov/wo/st/en.html
- Dig! The Archaeology Magazine for Kids, http://www.digonsite.com
- The Archaeology Channel, http://www.archaeologychannel.org

Sources: National Council for the Social Studies, 1994; National Council of Teachers of English and International Reading Association, 1996.

KEY THEMES

Developing excavation skills

Interpreting historic artifacts

Communicating explanations and interpretations

MATERIALS

Large plastic tubs or wood stakes and string

Sand

Various artifact replicas/objects (see procedure for suggestions)

Data sheets (provided)

Pens/pencils

Masking tape

Paint brushes

PROCEDURES

Begin by providing students with information about the work of archaeologists. You may find the two literature selections mentioned in this chapter to be helpful in this area. Video clips or images from the Internet or magazines can also be helpful. Sometimes students think archaeologists study dinosaurs. Be sure to let students know that archaeologists focus on human history!

As part of the preparation for the activity, you will want to share basic tools of an archaeologist with students. Many of these can be brought in as three-dimensional items. Others can be represented by color photos (see box below). As items are shared with students, encourage them to hypothesize how each might be used during an archaeological dig. Spend considerable time emphasizing the need to document every step of an excavation. Recording where something was discovered as well as what was discovered near the item can tell a researcher a lot about its use or role in that society.

An Archaeologist's Tools

Notebook

Pens/pencils

Maps/diagrams

Information sources (books about a culture)

Trowel or shallow shovel

Soft-bristled brushes

Cell phone

String

Small wooden stakes

Once students are familiar with the process of archaeological work, instruct them that they will be taking part in an archaeological dig on the school site. This is also a chance for discussion. Creating mini dig sites in large plastic tubs will have the least effect on the general school grounds. However, sectioning off a part of the schoolyard for a day and launching a full-scale archaeological dig with stakes and string marking off transects for study will not only lend authenticity, but it can lead into discussions of how actual digs may curtail activities in the area and prevent access to certain areas to the general population. Students can debate how to balance these competing priorities.

In designing your archaeological dig, you can bury any number of "artifacts." Replica arrowheads can be purchased very inexpensively from online suppliers. Inexpensive pots can be purchased from discount stores, smashed, and then the shards buried for students to not only locate but also to reassemble. You can include "charred" pieces of wood that might replicate a campfire, rusty metal items (safety first—no sharp edges!), shells, or even chicken bones that might represent a historic meal. You may chose to include "nonhistoric" items such as a bottle cap or plastic toy on top of the historic layers to prompt discussion of how to determine what to focus on during an excavation. Use whatever resources are available to create the dig site. It is okay to have mixed time period items; that can be part of the follow-up discussion!

Regardless of what is buried, what will most help create an authentic feel is by providing a grid system to facilitate recording the data. This will basically be a system of wooden posts and string that will create squares over the dig area. Each square should be lettered and numbered on the data sheet (see Figure 4.1 on p. 29). Students will record not only what they discover, but where they discover it, to reinforce the importance of context in archaeological discoveries. If small tubs are used, simply dividing the tub in halves or three triangles can replicate this system of data collection even in a small space.

After the dig is completed, students will participate in a grand discussion and share their discoveries with their peers. Topics should focus on what time period they feel these artifacts came from and why. In a true dig, the newer items will most likely be in the top layers, with older items in lower layers. It is often hard to replicate strict layers in the confines of a schoolyard. To work within this limitation, students might hypothesize that a disturbance such as building a playground (or in states like California, an earthquake!) may have altered the logical stratification. They might also enjoy trying to piece together the broken pot shards using masking tape to hold pieces together as they go. After the group discussion, have students complete the bottom part of the data sheet, recording specific data on one of the items that they recovered.

As a follow-up to the physical activity of the dig, lead a brief discussion about how students as citizens can best protect archaeological sites. After the group discussion, provide each student with a copy of the dilemma sheet (see Figure 4.2 on p. 30), and ask them to provide an individual response to the challenge.

GRADE-LEVEL MODIFICATIONS

K–2nd Grade

For younger students, unbroken artifacts that are easily identifiable will be the best choice. Limit the number of squares and place students in groups with a single recorder per group. For students with emerging literacy skills, lead a group discussion regarding the dilemma question rather than requiring written responses.

3rd Grade–5th Grade

These students should be able to participate in the activity as described previously. Students may need support in carefully excavating artifacts. This can be accomplished by arranging for two or three parent volunteers for the day of the activity or the support of a teaching assistant. If asking students to piece together pottery, incorporate large pieces. For dilemma narratives, expect responses in line with concrete thinking and with heavy emphasis on right and wrong. Support students in discovering gray areas of dilemmas through class discussion.

6th Grade–8th Grade

These students will benefit from detailed and extensive excavation sites. Groups of two will provide students with little downtime and plenty of activity to keep them on task. This group will be able to reassemble pottery with smaller shards and will be able to glean meaning from artifacts that are damaged, broken, or incomplete. Work with students at this grade level to articulate thoughtful responses to the proposed dilemma, taking into account multiple perspectives.

MEETING THE NEEDS OF ENGLISH LEARNERS

This activity incorporates a Total Physical Response approach that will specifically support English learners in engaging with and understanding the content. In addition, the tie to the multicultural context of archaeology studies will also support student learning. Last, the drawing component of the activity will allow English learners an alternative pathway outside of traditional narrative to communicate their discoveries. Additional modifications that can be made include providing a word bank for students to support completion of the written narrative of the assignment. Offering an alternative assessment option, such as allowing the student to orally explain the process of their excavation as well as the conclusions they have drawn may also prove helpful. If the class is predominantly English learners, discussion of the dilemmas can be completed orally rather than in written form.

MEETING THE NEEDS OF STUDENTS WITH SPECIAL NEEDS

The drawing component of the activity will be helpful for students with cognitive disabilities who may find authoring complex, narrative sentences difficult. Some students with gross motor difficulties may have difficulty working in a sandbox at ground level. Creating a portable box that can be used at desk-level will support these students. Selecting items that are robust will help prevent accidental breakage and will support students with limited fine motor abilities. Double-stick tape attached to the brush can help these students with grip and support their active participation.

Assessment Suggestion

At the conclusion of the activity, students will be able to:

- Record data using a grid system
- Recreate a historic scenario using data from artifacts
- Formulate opinions regarding preservation of historic sites and artifacts

Students' data sheets as well as their narrative responses to the dilemma can serve as assessment pieces.

Score	Data Sheet	Dilemma Response
4	All elements of the data sheet are complete and correct with detailed illustrations and descriptions.	Student provides a sound response to the dilemma that clearly reflects understanding of key archaeological principles.
3	Data sheet is mostly complete and mostly correct; small areas need improvement.	Student response is appropriate and supported.
2	Data sheet has some correct and complete elements, but with substantial incomplete sections or inaccuracies.	Student response is fairly reasonable but doesn't indicate a true understanding of the situation.
1	Data sheet has little completed or correct.	Student response is not appropriate.

Children's Literature Connection

Archaeologists Dig for Clues
   By Kate Duke
   ISBN: 978–0064451758
Archaeology (Kingfisher Knowledge)
   By Trevor Barnes and Tony Robinson
   ISBN: 978–0753461587
   These two works will provide students at different grade levels developmentally appropriate insight into the work of an archaeologist.

Quick Fact

There are several specialty fields related to archaeology. An archaeobotanist studies plant remains at an archaeological site to better understand the role plants played in a particular civilization. A geoarchaeologist studies the geography or geology of the area surrounding an archaeological site to further understanding of the site and its inhabitants. A zooarchaeologist studies animal remains in an archaeological site to determine details of diet or presence of companion animals.

FIGURE 4.1 Field Site Sample Data Sheet   K–2nd, 3rd–5th, 6th–8th

Researcher Name(s): _____ Date: _____

Field Site Location: _____

This is what we discovered:

	1	2	3	4	5	6	7	8	9	10
A										
B										
C										
D										
E										
F										
G										
H										
I										
J										

For my detailed observation, I chose an object I found in this location of the grid:. _____

These are some details I observed:

_____

_____

_____

_____

These are some additional things I'd like to know:

_____

_____

_____

_____

FIGURE 4.2   Archaeological Dilemma Sample Data Sheet   3rd–5th, 6th–8th

You are visiting your grandfather's ranch. He has a lot of land that you and your brother like to explore. While hiking around one day, you explore a cave and find a half-buried pot. It appears to be very old and may date back to the time when Native Americans lived in the area. What do you do?

- Leave the pot where it is and don't tell anyone.
- Try and dig it up by yourself.
- Make a map of where it is, and go tell your grandfather.
- Tell your grandfather, and ask if he will notify someone at the local university to help excavate it carefully.
- Ask your grandfather if you can sell it for extra spending money.
- Share the pot with the local museum.
- Other ideas?

I would:

_____

_____

_____

_____

I choose this response because:

_____

_____

_____

_____

REFERENCES

Canestrari, A. (2005). Social studies and geography: Beyond rote memorization. In R. H. Audet & L. K. Jordan (Eds.), *Integrating inquiry across the curriculum* (pp. 17–42). Thousand Oaks, CA: Corwin Press.

Covington, M. V. (1998). *The will to learn: A guide for motivating young people.* Cambridge, UK: Cambridge University Press.

Gardner, H. (1993). *Frames of mind: The theory of multiple intelligences.* Jackson, TN: Basic Books.

Glendinning, M. (2005). Digging into history: Authentic learning through archaeology. *History Teacher, 38,* 209–223.

Moe, J. M., Coleman, C., Fink, K., & Krejs, K. (2002). Archaeology, ethics, and character: Using our cultural heritage to teach citizenship. *The Social Studies, 93*(3), 109–113.

National Council for the Social Studies. (1994). *Expectations of excellence: Curriculum standards for social studies.* Washington, DC: Author.

National Council of Teachers of English and International Reading Association. (1996). *Standards for the English language arts.* Urbana, IL: National Council of Teachers of English.

Weaver, B., & Brown, C. (2003). Dig into archaeology. *Science Activities, 40*(3), 6–14.

Whitting, N. C. (1998). Archaeology and intercultural education in the elementary grades: An example from Minnesota. *The Social Studies, 89*(6), 254–259.

Images as Primary Sources

FAMILY PHOTO PROJECT

Yoji knew exactly what his assigned photograph meant. It was a picture of his classmate Crysta standing in front of door with a really clean outfit on. She had a new backpack at her feet, wore shiny shoes, and looked a little nervous. No one else was in the picture with her, but a tree could be seen in the background. The trees leaves were just beginning to change a little bit. They were in third grade now, but she looked about five or six in the picture. He could tell because she was missing one of her front teeth, and that's how old he was when he lost that tooth.

Yoji had a picture just like this one; that's how he knew what it meant. It was the first day of school. That's why everything was so new and why she looked so scared. His first day of school was in Japan, before he moved to the United States. Even though his clothes and backpack were different, he was also really nervous and looked just like Crysta did in her picture. "I guess everyone is nervous on the first day of school," he mumbled to himself.

The importance of primary sources has been established in earlier chapters. Photographs as primary sources can be especially engaging for students and simpler for primary students, English learners, and students with disabilities to use than primary sources that are primarily narrative text. Using personal photographs rather than stock photography can build concept understanding by supporting students by establishing a personal connection and demonstrating social science as relevant to students' everyday lives (Tanner, 2008).

One way to help students see the relevance of the school social studies curriculum is to make connections between standards and individual family history. Use of family artifacts and photos has shown as an extremely effective method to actively engage students with social studies content (Singer & Singer, 2004). Family and friend photos often depict cultural universals of meals, celebrations, homes, and relationships—experiences all students share. Emphasis on these cultural universals as part of the social studies curriculum supports a student's understanding of his or her own culture as well as the culture of others (Alleman, Knighton, & Brophy, 2007). Photos also provide students with the opportunity to share their own individual stories, an instructional method that has also proven successful in connecting with diverse learners while simultaneously building language arts skills (Lake, 2002).

Please visit www.sagepub.com/lmelberstudy for the updated National Council of the Social Studies standards.

Curriculum Standards for Social Studies

- Strand I: Culture
- Strand III: People, Places, & Environments
- Strand IV: Individual Development & Identity

Standards for the English Language Arts

Completing the data sheet builds writing skills, and discussing pictures with a partner supports oral language development.

- Standard 4:   Students adjust their use of spoken, written, and visual language (e.g., conventions, style, vocabulary) to communicate effectively with a variety of audiences and for different purposes.

- Standard 5:   Students employ a wide range of strategies as they write and use different writing process elements appropriately to communicate with different audiences for a variety of purposes.

Technology Connection

You may want to download images of families using a basic search to promote classroom discussion either in preparation for the activity or as a follow-up activity.

A helpful Web site is The Brownie Camera @ 100, http://www.kodak.com/US/en/corp/features/brownieCam/.

This site provides background on the development of the Kodak Brownie camera as well as firsthand accounts of the personal effect of the Kodak Brownie.

Sources: National Council for the Social Studies, 1994; National Council of Teachers of English and International Reading Association, 1996.

KEY THEMES

Analyzing photographs

Making inferences based on data

Sharing personal stories

MATERIALS

Data sheets (provided)

Photos of students (photocopies if possible)

Pens/pencils

PROCEDURES

Before beginning the activity, ensure that all students have access to a photo of themselves with family members or friends. Sometimes students who live with extended family or in foster care may not have photos handy. If this is the case, refer to the box below for suggestions on how to move forward with the activity in an inclusive manner.

Special Considerations

When doing this activity, it is important to be familiar with students' home lives. Students in foster care or a group-home setting may not have access to photos of family or friends. This can be easily remedied by snapping photos of the student on campus helping out a younger student, playing a sport, or eating lunch with friends well in advance of the activity. These photos can quietly be provided to the student as an option to use for the activity. While it will most likely not be possible to take photos of all children in the class, it is more likely that only one or two students will need you to step in and provide these images.

Also, avoid creating matching games in which students try and connect an early photo with a classmate. These types of activities often single out students who may be physically or culturally different from their peers in a way that is uncomfortable for the student.

Once it has been determined that all students are likely to have access to a photo of themselves engaged in an activity, send a letter home to families asking to use a family photo in a class activity (see Figure 5.1 on p. 36). Provide guidelines as to the type of photo that is needed. Simple school portraits will not work as there is no context for students to study. Rather, it is important that the photos show other individuals, pets, or a location in the background for discussion. I usually put additional regulations that images should not show nudity (i.e., no "toddler in the bath" shots) or alcohol use.

Well in advance of the activity, make color copies of each photo, and note its owner on the back. Many home printers can now make color copies with little ink use. To do this, simply place as many photos as can fit on the glass (often four) and make a single copy. Local office supply stores also have reasonable prices, and again, multiple photos can fit on a single page. If copying the photos is not an option, the activity can still be done. Photos can be affixed to the data sheet by tape on the back and carefully detached after display to be returned.

The first part of the activity should focus on the work of social scientists and the role of photographs as primary sources. Share a photo with students and hold a group discussion asking students what they think the photo tells them about the lives of the people in the photo. This discussion should focus on cultural universals or things that all people share. Examples include home, food, family and friends, or fun. Most people in the world have some type of home or dwelling, be it temporary or permanent. What do these have in common? How are they different? We all rely on food, although different cultures may prefer different diets.

For the second part of the activity, students will be assigned a photo of one of their classmates. To facilitate the later discussion, it is most efficient to have two students swap photos so when it is time for discussion, pairs are predetermined. They will use an open-ended data sheet to record their thoughts on what is happening in the picture (see Figure 5.2 on p. 37). Is it a holiday celebration? Are a brother and sister fighting over a toy? Is someone learning how to ride a bike for the first time? To support student analysis, it may be helpful to list several of the following focus questions on the chalkboard:

- Who is in the picture?
- How do you think the people in the photo are related or connected?
- What can you tell me about what the people are doing?
- Are there objects in the photo that tell you something about the people?
- What do you notice about the background of the photo?
- Can you determine where the photo was taken?
- Is there anything in the photo that tells you when it might have been taken?
- Is there anything missing from the photo that you would expect to see?

Have students record their thoughts on the data sheet. They will then meet with the person who brought in the picture and share these thoughts. The owner of the photo will then provide the other student with the actual story, and the two can discuss any similarities or differences between the inferences and fact. When both sections of the data sheet are completed, the photocopy of the picture can be affixed to the data sheet, and the final products posted in the classroom on a class bulletin board.

A whole-class discussion should then be held to debrief students. What were they able to discern just from looking at the photos? What types of things were impossible for them to know? Did any students make any incorrect assumptions? What led to those inaccuracies? This activity can be replicated several times during the year to build observation and inference skills.

GRADE-LEVEL MODIFICATIONS

K–2nd Grade

For younger students, this activity can be modified and completed as a group. Rather than having students review the photographs individually, the teacher will share an enlarged image in front of the whole class and lead the discussion outlined previously. This can be done by scanning and enlarging the photo using a home computer, using an LCD projector to project a scanned image, or using a digital visual presenter. If this technology is not available, multiple copies of the image can be made at its regular size, and students can handle their own copy of the image as the discussion takes place. Second-grade students are likely to be able to conduct the activity as it is described but with the support of a word bank or assistance with writing.

3rd Grade–5th Grade

These students should be able to participate in the activity as described previously. Students of this age may need to be reminded about being polite and treating each other with respect. It is okay to laugh at an image that is intended to be funny such as a baby with cake on his or her face or a puppy misbehaving. However, it will be important to review that students may observe lifeways that are different than their own and that respect for these differences is important.

6th Grade–8th Grade

These students will also benefit from a discussion on respecting differences, as this grade range can be a hotbed for teasing. To avoid inappropriate discussions, or questions or inferences that might prove embarrassing, a more detailed data sheet guiding the analysis can be implemented if there is concern about students being respectful. Older students can conduct analysis with an eye for deciphering even more detail by dividing the photo into quadrants. By dividing the photograph into sections and asking students to carefully look section by section, new details become apparent that can further support content analysis.

MEETING THE NEEDS OF ENGLISH LEARNERS

With its emphasis on visuals and activating the prior knowledge of students, this cooperative group activity already contains several elements that make it a good match for the needs of English learners. Additional modifications might include students sharing their discoveries orally rather than through written narrative, modifying the length requirement of the assignment to support students in focusing on a few key facts, or providing a word bank.

MEETING THE NEEDS OF STUDENTS WITH SPECIAL NEEDS

This activity is already well designed to meet the needs of students with disabilities. Students with cognitive delays or learning disabilities will find the concrete relevance of the activity supports their content acquisition. The collaborative component is also a helpful component for these students. Viewing photos should not be something that poses difficulty for students with physical disabilities. For students who have low vision, a large magnifier will help them view details in the different photographs. For students who are blind, an audio description of the picture can be prepared and recorded on a portable tape recorder, or the student can select a peer to describe the image to him or her.

ASSESSMENT SUGGESTION

At the conclusion of the activity, students will be able to:

- Draw inferences based on collected data
- Effectively glean information from primary sources
- Adjust findings based on additional information

Students' final presentation boards can be assessed using the following rubric:

Score	Content Criteria	Presentation Criteria
4	Project contains detailed, clear information in all four areas.	Project is very well organized, is neatly completed, and demonstrates the highest effort.
3	Project contains information in all four areas although it is limited in details.	Project is of acceptable quality.
2	Project contains information in fewer than four areas with acceptable details.	Project lacks neatness and demonstrates a lack of organizational effort.
1	Project contains minimal information.	Project demonstrates minimal effort.

Children's Literature Connection

Family Pictures/Cuadros de Familia
  By Pat Mora
  ISBN: 978–0892392063
  This brilliantly illustrated work supports students in "reading" the stories told by pictures of family events and celebrations.

Quick Fact

Older students may be interested to know that during the 1800s, many families could not afford to take photographs of loved ones. For these families, it was common that the only photos they had of family members were provided after their death and free of charge by funeral parlors. The invention of the Kodak Brownie camera in 1900 provided the means for anyone to take inexpensive photos and preserve family memories.

FIGURE 5.1 Sample Family Letter: Family Photo Project

Dear Family Member,

We are learning about families and our community as part of our social studies curriculum. We will need each child to bring a photograph of himself or herself with either family or friends. The photograph will not be harmed and will be returned in a few days. During the project, your child will share the photo with his or her classmates and talk about what is happening in the picture. The photograph may be a recent one or may have been taken some time ago.

   Any photo is acceptable as long as your child is in it. We do ask that photos not have alcohol or tobacco use by adults or be focused on bath time or potty training. Other than that, anything goes!

   Please let me know if you have questions. If you don't have easy access to family photos, please let me know, and I will be happy to snap a picture of your child with his or her friends here at school.

Sincerely,

Mrs. Smith

FIGURE 5.2 Family Photo Analysis Sample Data Sheet   K–2nd, 3rd–5th, 6th–8th

Historian: _____

Date: _____

[blank box]

My analysis:

_____

_____

_____

_____

_____

_____

Photograph owner's response:

_____

_____

_____

_____

_____

_____

_____

REFERENCES

Alleman, J., Knighton, B., & Brophy, J. (2007). Social studies: Incorporating all children using community and cultural universals as the centerpiece. *Journal of Learning Disabilities, 40,* 166–173.

Lake, V. (2002). Including their voices: Storytelling by children. *Social Studies and the Young Learner, 14*(4), 24–26.

National Council for the Social Studies. (1994). *Expectations of excellence: Curriculum standards for social studies.* Washington, DC: Author.

National Council of Teachers of English and International Reading Association. (1996). *Standards for the English language arts.* Urbana, IL: National Council of Teachers of English.

Singer, J. Y., & Singer, A. J. (2004). Creating a museum of family artifacts. *Social Studies and the Young Learner, 17*(5), 5–10.

Tanner, L. (2008). No Child Left Behind is just the tip of the iceberg. *The Social Studies, 99*(1), 41–45.

UNIT II
Connecting to Community

Connecting to the community can be a valuable way for elementary students of all ages to relate to social studies skills, concepts, values, and attitudes (Committee on Developments in the Science of Learning, 1999). Connecting to their immediate environment promotes a personal relationship with knowledge and understanding. This knowledge and understanding can lead to further analysis and evaluation of how one's community developed and the reasons for its current status.

Teachers can use various activities to stimulate interest in and learning about the community. Students can be asked to identify significant changes. They draw and create maps as well as do fieldwork that helps describe current status. Community service or service learning can help learners make their community a better place (Committee on Developments in the Science of Learning, 1999). Actual and virtual field trips can help elementary learners expand their local environment as they relate to sites outside of their immediate environment.

REFERENCE

Committee on Developments in the Science of Learning. (1999). *How people learn: Brain, mind, experience, and school* (J. D. Bransford, A. L. Brown, & R. R. Cockney, Eds.). Washington, DC: National Academies Press.

Strategy 6

Personally Relevant History

EXPLORING COMMUNITY HISTORY

The teacher was taking the class for a walk in their neighborhood.

"That's my grandmother's house," said John. "She's lived in that house since she was a little girl."

"I wonder what it was like when she was a little girl," joins in Maria.

"One day, she told me a story about her life when she was young," continued John. "She told about how the street wasn't so wide and the cars were bigger. There were no large stores, and her mother would give her a nickel when she came home from school to go to the store on the corner and buy her favorite—a pickle!"

"How silly!" said Carlos, "I wonder where that store is?"

"And what else has changed in our town!" Maria added.

Studying the changes in the community where one lives can be an exciting and very personal adventure. Young students can get to discover what the community was like by combing through historical records, reading personal letters, talking to those of an older generation, looking at old high school yearbooks, and many other ways. Teachers can obtain any of these resources by working with a local historical society, speaking with older citizens, consulting newspaper archives, and purchasing pictures and postcards at flea markets and sales. Students can then be challenged to use these resources to compare what they discovered to what exists today.

This comparison of the past to today can cause students to reflect on how and why people create and change their towns to continually meet the needs of the inhabitants. It can cause them to think about how forces outside of the community have affected the town.

- Was the area a victim of any natural disasters, such as floods, hurricanes, earthquakes, and so forth?
- Was the town built around a factory that employed much of the local community?
- Was the community founded by a particular family or group of people?

Studying photographs depicting a town during years past can be particularly interesting for young students. These photographs are truly artifacts of a former time, place, and people. Comparing these visual images to those of today can provide learners with a way to look at each time period and make conclusions. What was life like during each time period? How has life in the community changed from the older photograph to the one from today?

Van Horn (2008) beautifully describes the rich experiences that can be gained from examining photographs. She writes, "Photographs are texts in that they hold messages within their borders. The elements in a photograph—are the 'words' of the text. A viewer, or 'reader,' examines the elements or 'words' within the frame" (p. 4).

Sources: National Council for the Social Studies, 1994; National Council of Teachers of English and International Reading Association, 1996.

Please visit www.sagepub.com/lmelberstudy for the updated National Council of the Social Studies standards.

Curriculum Standards for Social Studies

- Strand II: Time, Continuity, & Change
- Strand III: People, Places, & Environment
- Strand IV: Individual Development & Identity

Standards for the English Language Arts

Students develop writing and oral language skills through the analysis process.

- Standard 1:   Students read a wide range of print and nonprint texts to build an understanding of texts, of themselves, and of the cultures of the United States and the world; to acquire new information; to respond to the needs and demands of society and the workplace; and for personal fulfillment. Among these texts are fiction and nonfiction, classic and contemporary works.

- Standard 3:   Students apply a wide range of strategies to comprehend, interpret, evaluate, and appreciate texts. They draw on their prior experience, their interactions with other readers and writers, their knowledge of word meaning and of other texts, their word identification strategies, and their understanding of textual features (e.g., sound–letter correspondence, sentence structure, context, graphics).

Technology Connection

Students can use the Internet to locate historic images of their town and even search virtual archives. They may want to create a class Web site with historic images of community sites paired with modern images taken with a digital camera.

KEY THEMES

Making observations

Analyzing pictures

Comparing and contrasting

Inferring from visual images

Hypothesizing

MATERIALS

Teachers need to search for and collect pictures of the community in the past. Using Internet resources, in addition to finding old photographs and postcards, can yield productive results. Teachers should look for images that depict scenes rather than people. This will make it easier for learners to relate the pictures to images from today. Cameras are also needed so that learners can take snapshots of the scene as it looks now. It is not necessary to have a camera for each student. Groups can be formed to work collaboratively to take various pictures of the same scene. Groups could also be formed so members can share the same camera and give each other advice as they take pictures of various individual sites.

PROCEDURES

This activity is grounded in educating students in an appreciation of photography as an art form. First, teachers present an enlarged photograph the whole class can easily see. Instruction on how to look at a picture begins with asking the students to tell what they see in the picture. As they brainstorm, teachers record these comments.

Next the students are taught to look at the picture using the four-quadrants approach as a way to analyze what the picture is really about. The teacher physically divides the picture into four quadrants. The entire class can discuss what they see in the first quadrant (upper left), proceed to the second quadrant (upper right), analyze the third quadrant (lower left), and end with the fourth quadrant (lower right; see Figure 6.1 on p. 45). The class also could be divided into groups to look at only one quadrant and then complete a "jigsaw" as each quadrant group reports on its analysis. Teachers should lead the class to consider how what students saw when they viewed the picture as a whole has been refined and expanded as they examined each section. Guiding questions for the examination of the photograph as a whole or the quadrants can include:

- What do you see? Use lots of detail in your descriptions.
- Are there trees, roads, cars, houses, churches, monuments, or buildings in the picture?
- Can you guess about what year or time period the photograph was taken? Why did you guess as you did?
- Does the image look familiar—like any place you already know?

After the class examination of the old photograph, teachers should tell the learners what the photograph actually depicts as well as how the place or site looks today. In addition, showing them the modern photograph or taking them to the site of the picture can be a great surprise and lead to a class discussion about how and why the change has occurred. Perhaps change was due to human interaction or even to natural disasters occurring.

Each student or group of students should be given an old photograph of a different location or neighborhood in the community. Examination of this artifact will be done through the quadrant method as students try to figure out the location. Students should share their best guesses, and then teachers reveal the actual locations. Cameras can be provided so that the learners can take pictures of the modern site. Although getting them to the sites might be tricky, there are options to consider. Parents can be enlisted to take students after school to do the picture taking, a bus trip can be arranged, or the whole class can walk to the site.

Once students have taken their pictures, they should compare them with the older photographs. Beginning by examining their own picture through the quadrant method, they should then compare what they see with the other image. After this, the teacher should lead a class discussion about changes in the community that were discovered by comparing and contrasting the new and old photographs. Why might these changes have occurred?

GRADE-LEVEL MODIFICATIONS

K–2nd Grade

Young learners will delight in this activity. There are digital cameras available that are easy for them to use because they are geared for this age group. Students should be given plenty of practice on using the cameras before they venture out to take the "now" pictures. Teachers may also choose to take the pictures themselves. They may narrow the scope of the activity so that it is a whole-class project with one or a few pictures compared together as a class. The activity can be tailored so that it relates to sites closest to the students such as school or home.

3rd Grade–5th Grade

Students of this age group likewise will enjoy taking pictures for a class activity. They can be challenged to write a short story about being alive during the time of the first photograph and explaining what they did in school, what they did to have fun, what was their town like, who was their family, and so forth. Another short story topic is to write about being alive during the time of the first photo and being suddenly transported to the picture from today.

6th Grade–8th Grade

After these learners view the older picture, they can be challenged to draw what they think the scene looks like today. Then they can go to the scene and see how accurate their depiction is. They would still use cameras to take photographs of the present-day location. Students could be asked to then write an essay comparing and contrasting the two images. This essay should include reasons why they believe the changes between the two photographs took place. Outside research might be required to complete this assignment.

MEETING THE NEEDS OF ENGLISH LEARNERS

This activity promotes visual literacy and competence in all learners. Students who are learning English can be successful even if they do not have fluent writing skills. They can talk about each picture and the relationship between the images. Talking translation dictionaries can be provided to assist learners with new vocabulary to use in speaking and writing.

MEETING THE NEEDS OF STUDENTS WITH SPECIAL NEEDS

Visual literacy and competence are stressed in this activity. Students with learning disabilities that affect writing and reading competencies can excel. They can speak about their pictures and create their own illustrations to depict the original as well as the newer scene. Then they can draw a representation of how the image has changed. For students with visual concerns, it might be necessary to use technology to enlarge the pictures. An LCD projector can be attached to a computer to enlarge the image. A CCTV (closed circuit television) can also be used to enlarge pictures, and this aid has the capability to adjust the level of magnification to meet students' needs.

ASSESSMENT SUGGESTION

At the conclusion of this activity, students will be able to:

- Analyze photographs in a deliberate manner that encourages visual literacy and competence
- Compare and contrast images from different time periods
- Make inferences about the causes of differences

Students' data sheets will be assessed using the following rubric:

Score	Criteria
4	All sections of the assignment are complete with exceptional detail and insight; comparisons and contrasts are clearly delineated and explained.
3	All sections are complete with an acceptable level of detail; comparisons and contrasts are delineated and explained.
2	Most of the sections are complete with an acceptable level of detail or some sections are complete but have errors; comparisons and contrasts are incomplete or not evident.
1	Most of the sections are incomplete or inaccurate; little or no evidence of comparison and contrast.

Children's Literature Connection

A City Through Time
   By DK Publishing
   ISBN: 0756606411
   This picture book tells the story of the history and growth of a city.

A Port Through Time
   By Anne Millard, DK Children
   ISBN: 140531267X
   This volume tells the story of how a port city changed through time from a settlement to a large-scale port.

A Street Through Time
  By Anne Millard
  ISBN: 0789434261
  This book uses pictures to show how a street evolved. The artwork is busy but interesting.

Quick Fact

The first urban settlements or "communities" can be traced to around 3,000 B.C. in ancient Mesopotamia, Egypt, and the Indus Valley. Ancient cities were typically walled for defense.

FIGURE 6.1   Sample Data Sheet   All Grade Levels

Part I: Examining the Older Image

 1. What do you see in this picture?
    _____
    _____
    _____
    _____

 2. Look at the picture again.
    What do you see in the upper left-hand quadrant?
    _____
    _____
    _____
    _____

    What do you see in the upper right-hand quadrant?
    _____
    _____
    _____
    _____

    What do you see in the lower left-hand quadrant?
    _____
    _____
    _____
    _____

    What do you see in the lower right-hand quadrant?
    _____
    _____
    _____
    _____

(Continued)

FIGURE 6.1   (Continued)   All Grade Levels

Part II: Examining the New Picture

    1. What do you see in this picture?

_____

_____

_____

_____

    2. Why did you take this picture as your did?

_____

_____

_____

_____

    3. Look at the picture again.
       What do you see in the upper left-hand quadrant?

_____

_____

_____

_____

       What do you see in the upper right-hand quadrant?

_____

_____

_____

_____

       What do you see in the lower left-hand quadrant?

_____

_____

_____

_____

       What do you see in the lower right-hand quadrant?

_____

_____

_____

_____

Part III: Comparison and Contrast

    1. What do these two pictures have in common?

_____

_____

_____

_____

2. How are these two pictures different?

_____

_____

_____

_____

3. Why do you think there are differences between the two pictures?

_____

_____

_____

_____

4. What changes in the community may be related to these differences?

_____

_____

_____

_____

REFERENCES

National Council for the Social Studies. (1994). *Expectations of excellence: Curriculum standards for social studies*. Washington, DC: Author.

National Council of Teachers of English and International Reading Association. (1996). *Standards for the English language arts*. Urbana, IL: National Council of Teachers of English.

VanHorn, L. (2008). *Reading photographs to write with meaning and purpose*. Newark, DE: International Reading Association.

Strategy
7

Developing Map Skills

NEIGHBORHOOD EXPLORATION

"You know what I wonder about, Lorelei?" shared Alton. "I worry that I will get lost on my way to school. I worry that I will get lost in this big school building."

"I saw my dad look up something on the Internet, and it told him how to get from my house to New Jersey. He said he would not get lost because now he had directions and a map so we could get to Grandma's really quick," answered Lorelei.

"I guess we could ask the teacher how to make a map so we would not get lost on our way to school or in this big building. What do you think, Lorelei?" responded Alton.

Developing map skills in elementary students can help them as they explore and understand their own neighborhood and school. Sunal and Haas (2005) maintain that "one of the best ways to learn the definition of a map is to make your own maps" (p. 313). These same authors advise teachers to assist the youngest learners by exposing them to maps with few symbols and having them create their own simple maps. The reading and creating of maps should inspire elementary students to think of themselves not only as part of their neighborhood but also as part of a community, the nation, and the world.

Parker (2009) identifies five different skills essential for understanding maps and mapping: (1) directional orientation, (2) map scales, (3) place location, (4) location expression, and (5) map symbols. Directional orientation refers to whether a learner understands the concepts of near and far as well as north, south, east, and west. When asked to point to the north, many elementary students point above their heads and point to the south as the floor. Teachers need to clarify directional orientation as it applies to a flat map. Map scales relate to the fact that mathematics is an essential skill relating to producing a scale—that is, translating something from a larger size to a smaller one. Place location for younger students relates to helping them see how the places they already know can be represented on a map. For older elementary students, place location refers to using a grid to locate locations by identifying coordinates. Location expression means that learners are able to reference one locale to another. In other words, where is the school in relation to their home? Where is their best friend's home in relation to their home? Finally, young learners need to be taught how the sites and locations that they know can be transformed into symbols that make sense to them on a map representation.

Asking elementary school students to create their own maps of the places they know can help them understand all of the map skills that they need to know. This exploration can be as expansive as exploring their own neighborhood or be as personally relevant as mapping their school, classroom, home, or a room in their home.

Sources: National Council for the Social Studies, 1994; National Council of Teachers of English and International Reading Association, 1996.

Please visit www.sagepub.com/lmelberstudy for the updated National Council of the Social Studies standards.

Curriculum Standards for Social Studies

- Strand III: People, Places, & Environments
- Strand IV: Individual Development & Identity

Standards for the English Language Arts

The research process and completing their own maps will build vocabulary as well as support reaching comprehension skills. Students researching historic maps and conducting research to create their own maps will support reading comprehension as well as building new vocabulary.

- Standard 3:   Students apply a wide range of strategies to comprehend, interpret, evaluate, and appreciate texts. They draw on their prior experience, their interactions with other readers and writers, their knowledge of word meaning and of other texts, their word identification strategies, and their understanding of textual features (e.g., sound–letter correspondence, sentence structure, context, graphics).

- Standard 4:   Students adjust their use of spoken, written, and visual language (e.g., conventions, style, vocabulary) to communicate effectively with a variety of audiences and for different purposes.

- Standard 10:   Students whose first language is not English make use of their first language to develop competency in the English language arts and to develop understanding of content across the curriculum.

Technology Connection

Most of us have discovered that online mapping programs can be a great help in locating local addresses or even planning a trip across the country. Students may decide to compare their map with those available on the Internet. They may want to map out a fantasy trip in line with other topics of study.

KEY THEMES

Making observations of known places

Translating personal observations to generalizations

Communicating observations to others

Analyzing data to create maps

MATERIALS

Construction paper

Gridded paper (for older students)

Markers/pencils/colored pencils

Pads

Clipboards

PROCEDURES

This activity involves learners exploring known places. More important, it involves the production of maps that are related to students' own needs and experiences. The teacher should decide, depending on the age of the students and the location of the school, which explorations are most relevant and possible as well as how simple or complex the maps produced by the learners should be. Students should then be paired or grouped. Pairing or grouping works well for this activity when learners are asked about what they are interested in exploring and mapping, and teachers assign groups based on these indications. The contents of the map to be produced will be based on what has already been taught. For example, younger students should concentrate on directions (north, south, etc.) and map symbols (such as drawing a flag to represent their school). Location expression is also important for these learners to consider the concepts of "near," "far," "next to," and so forth. Older learners should construct their maps not only to include the ideas considered by younger learners but also to indicate scale and place location. Grid paper will facilitate production of maps that include number and letter grids.

Before beginning their explorations, students should be exposed to reading, analyzing, and talking about maps related to what they are studying in social studies. Students can compare and contrast maps from different time periods or different types of maps. Teachers should also model the construction of a map or have the class create a map collaboratively. An ideal way to construct this model map is to have learners individually draw a map of their classroom and then collaborate to produce a class map of the room.

Teachers can then lead the class on a map walk. Mapping the school can begin at a central location, such as a memorial plaque indicating when the school was built, and end at their classroom. Students can decide on what symbols will indicate offices, the lunch room, the gym, and so forth. They can also be given freedom as to what they decide is relevant for them to indicate on their maps (see Figure 7.1 on p. 53). The maps can be constructed as students walk, or the walk can be an opportunity for pre-drawing and the students' maps can be refined back in the classroom.

Map walking does not have to be confined to the school building. After getting the required permissions, teachers can extend the walk to the school's neighborhood, a local park, or another relevant community location.

GRADE-LEVEL MODIFICATIONS

K–2nd Grade

This age group can begin their mapping by working with their families to create a map of their home. This might be of their room, another room in their home, or even the entire house. This family involvement will help all students create a product that they are proud of and that is personally relevant to them, even those who have difficulty writing or drawing. Teachers can also create a basic map of the street where the school is located and use this device to teach the concepts of relative location—near, far, and so forth. Creating the map based on the map walk can be a whole-class activity guided by the teacher's drawing. Also, this map can be created on a felt board so that learners can physically place pieces to represent streets, the school, and locations that they as a class think are important.

3rd Grade–5th Grade

This activity can be presented as an interdisciplinary activity for students of this age group. After appropriate instruction, math concepts such as drawing to scale can be a required element to be included on the finished map. In addition, the map walk can be amplified to include a math walk in which students look for relevant math concepts. They can be asked to record ideas such as:

- How many steps does it take to get from one location to another?
- How many math shapes (triangles, trapezoids, etc.) did they see?

Teachers can first demonstrate and then require learners to include these interdisciplinary connections on their maps. Further classroom discussion can include geometric concepts as students identify streets that are parallel or perpendicular to each other.

6th Grade–8th Grade

Constructing a grid of letters and numbers as the basic structure for student maps can be a challenging yet relevant approach for this age group. This gridding allows them to understand how to locate significant places, such as hospitals, and how to travel from one point to another. These learners can also be asked to construct maps with a purpose or audience in mind. They could draw maps for people new to their town or for their younger brothers or sisters. Furthermore, they could be challenged to consider how to construct maps for individuals with low vision. The importance of clear and descriptive titles can also be a required focus for this age group.

- What exactly does the map contain?
- Why was the map created?
- What does what the map indicate about the group of students who created it?
- What does it tell the reader about what the creators considered important?

MEETING THE NEEDS OF ENGLISH LEARNERS

Teachers need to be sure that directions for completion of the activity are well understood. Vocabulary terms and concepts, such as gridding, need to be demonstrated and displayed. Visual guidance, such as large, teacher-created maps, can be used to model each concept of mapping that the students are required to know. In addition, all students in the class can be required to incorporate languages other than English in their map legends, street names, and place names.

MEETING THE NEEDS OF STUDENTS WITH SPECIAL NEEDS

How the maps are created and what the maps look like can be easily tailored to meet the needs and abilities of diverse learners. Some may choose to produce their maps with the aid of computers. Others can dictate what they would like to create to a peer or adult helper. A map handout can be provided with larger print or more details to further guide learners with low vision.

ASSESSMENT SUGGESTION

At the conclusion of the activity, students will be able to:

- Understand important concepts relating to map reading
- Apply these concepts to creation of a local map that is relevant to themselves, their classmates, and other community members

Students' maps can be assessed using a simple yes/no rubric centered on teachers' expectations and what is developmentally appropriate for the learner and age group. This rubric should be shared with learners prior to the assignment so that they understand fully the criteria and requirements.

Possible rubric for third- to fifth-grade map:

	Yes	No
Map clearly shows locations that the group considers important.		
Map shows that students understood all map concepts learned in class.		
Map is drawn to scale.		
The symbols on the map are clearly explained by the map's legend.		
Map can be used easily by classmates to identify places or to go from location to location.		

Children's Literature Connection

Although these books are not specifically about map making, they can be used by teachers as a way to demonstrate the importance of and interactions of people, places, and environments. In addition, students, as they read, can construct maps of the main characters' journeys.

Fort Chipewyan Homecoming: A Journey to Native Canada
   By Morningstar Mercredi
   ISBN: 0822597314
   This is the true story of a mother journeying with her son to Canada to introduce him to her culture. It is a photo-documentary that can help learners see the connection of people and environment and also can help them examine the complexity of parent and child relationships.

Grandfather's Journey
   By Allen Say
   ISBN: 0547076800

This beautifully illustrated book has become a classic to use to talk to young students about the meaning of home and places and the immigrant experience.

In the Woods: Who's Been Here

By Lindsay Barrett George

ISBN: 0688161634

This engaging book is appropriate for the younger learners. Teachers can use it as a guideline to make interdisciplinary connections with social studies and science walks.

Quick Fact

In the 1400s, Prince Henry of Portugal founded a school for sea captains so that they could study the best maps available at the time. This ruler has become known as Prince Henry the Navigator because historians consider the school he founded and the maps he collected as essential for the exploration of the world and early European travels to North America.

FIGURE 7.1   Exploring the School Sample Data Sheet   3rd–5th, 6th–8th

On the walk . . .

Our walk begins at the plaque that tells about when our school was built. List three facts contained on this plaque.

1. _____

2. _____

3. _____

How will you show this location on your map?

As we continue our walk, decide as a group which three other locations you will include on your map. Tell why these locations are important.

We want to include: _____ because . . .

_____

_____

We want to include: _____ because . . .

_____

_____

We want to include: _____ because . . .

_____

_____

(Continued)

FIGURE 7.1   (Continued)   3rd–5th, 6th–8th

As we walk, decide how you will indicate distance or scale on your map.

_____

_____

_____

Back in the classroom . . .

What symbols will you use for your map?

_____ = _____

_____ = _____

_____ = _____

_____ = _____

What materials will you use to create your map?

_____

_____

_____

How will you all work together to complete your map?

_____

_____

_____

_____

Preparing to present . . .

Get ready to present your map to your class. Talk about what you learned from this experience and how this might help you complete another map project in the future. What are some other maps you'd like to create?

_____

_____

_____

_____

REFERENCES

National Council for the Social Studies. (1994). *Expectations of excellence: Curriculum standards for social studies.* Washington, DC: Author.

National Council of Teachers of English and International Reading Association. (1996). *Standards for the English language arts.* Urbana, IL: National Council of Teachers of English.

Parker, W. C. (2009). *Social studies in elementary education.* Upper Saddle River, NJ: Prentice Hall.

Sunal, C. S., & Haas, M. E. (2005). *Social studies for the elementary and middle grades: A constructivist approach* (2nd ed.). Boston: Allyn & Bacon.

Connecting With Cultural Institutions

Strategy 8

LEARNING HISTORY THROUGH FIELD TRIPS

"I am so excited," said Lisa. "Tomorrow our class is going to what our teacher calls a living museum. I think it is a farm where they do things like they did really long ago."

"Gee, that sounds like fun," replied Scott. "I guess you will see cows and other animals. I wonder what will be different than a farm today?"

"Don't worry. I will tell you about it," responded Lisa.

"You know what? A lot of times our teacher takes us on 'virtual trips.' We get on the computers and travel to a lot of different places. It is really neat, and we don't even miss lunch or recess at school," commented Scott.

Field trips are a time honored and valuable part of the social studies curriculum as they help learners have relevant and real experiences relating to what they are studying in their classrooms. However, some teachers find it difficult to elevate these experiences to include critical thinking that reinforces, clarifies, and amplifies classroom learning (Bamberger & Tal, 2007). For the most successful field trip experience, Chapin (2005) encourages teachers to know what they want to achieve through the field trip, to focus students' attention during the trip, and to provide post-trip follow-up activities.

Of course, teachers must follow all school guidelines with regard such aspects as permission slips, number of chaperones, and special medical and dietary needs of students. Will the students return in time to take the school bus home? When will learners eat lunch? However, it is also important that teachers know the procedures and policies for the place visited. Are cameras permitted? Will a personal guide be assigned to groups of students or to the whole class? Will the guide be experienced in working with students of the class's age group? It is preferable that teachers actually visit the site prior to the class expedition and many field trip destinations provide free admission for educators to support this pre-visit planning. If a visit before the trip is not possible, teachers can learn more about the site by visiting the location's Web site or by contacting the facility in advance.

Prior to the field trip, teachers need to work with the students so they will understand what they will see, how they are expected to behave, and how the trip relates to what they are studying. Parker (2009) suggests using the K-W-L (know, want to know, and learned) activity to assess what students already know about the place to be visited. This activity can also be extended to include what students know and want to know about behavioral expectations. Learners can be asked to use this activity to speculate on how the trip relates to the curriculum and question themselves on what they want to learn from the field trip. Finally, the K-W-L strategy provides a post-trip activity as pupils complete the chart to record what they have learned. Teachers can lead discussions to have classes think critically and connect what they wanted to know and what they did learn. Most specifically, class discussions can revolve around how the field trip confirmed what was presented in the curriculum prior to the trip. Students may also consider how what they saw caused them to question what they had previously learned or raised new questions for exploration.

During the field trip, providing students with either specific questions or a central focus to guide their experience is essential. These questions and the manner of recording their answers should be explained prior to the actual day of the trip. Some teachers involve their students in creating the questions that the class feels are important to answer. Others, during their pre–field trip personal visit, develop trip data sheets that relate to specific elements of the location. Students need to be told if they will be expected to write answers to questions during the trip or will be asked to remember information for future classroom discussions (see Figure 8.1 on p. 60). It is important that as teachers generate questions to be answered during the trip, that they remember that the primary purpose of the trip should not be to answer only basic knowledge and comprehension questions but also to extend this knowledge and comprehension. Analysis, synthesis, and evaluation questions will assist the participants in relating the field trip to classroom learning and their own personal experiences. Data sheets that focus on an exhibit or experience rather than label text are most supportive of an inquiry-based experience (Kisiel, 2003). It is also important to note that carefully planned field trips can be successful without the use of data sheets. Including small-group discussion, use of photo-documentation, or reporting to adult chaperones are all methods of providing focus (Melber, 2008a).

Virtual field trips—using the Internet to explore places that are too far or expensive to actually visit—have become increasing popular as ways to electronically expand students' opportunities. The guidelines for an actual field trip apply to these visits also. Teachers should provide learners with pre-trip clarifications and expectations.

Sunal and Haas (2005) further contend that teachers should provide written directions of how the learners are to use the Web site. Modeling by teachers of how to use the site can be crucial. Allowing students to work in groups or pairs can also facilitate site navigation and a successful virtual field trip experience. Teachers should note that some virtual field trip sites require a fee or donation for full participation on the site.

Please visit www.sagepub.com/lmelberstudy for the updated National Council of the Social Studies standards.

Curriculum Standards for Social Studies

- Strand II: Time, Continuity, & Change
- Strand III: People, Places, & Environments
- Strand VII: Production, Distribution, & Consumption

Sources: National Council for the Social Studies, 1994; National Council of Teachers of English and International Reading Association, 1996.

Standards for the English Language Arts

By conducting interviews and completing data sheets students are utilizing a variety of language arts skills throughout the activity.

- Standard 7:   Students conduct research on issues and interests by generating ideas and questions, and by posing problems. They gather, evaluate, and synthesize data from a variety of sources (e.g., print and nonprint texts, artifacts, people) to communicate their discoveries in ways that suit their purpose and audience.

- Standard 12: Students use spoken, written, and visual language to accomplish their own purposes (e.g., for learning, enjoyment, persuasion, and the exchange of information).

Technology Connection

Many field trip destinations have online versions of their exhibits, downloadable curriculum for use by teachers, and even video clips that can bring the field trip destination into the classroom. Conducting a "virtual trip" can be another option for schools that may not be able to visit the site in person.

KEY THEMES

Making observations

Collecting data

Distinguishing important from less important information

Comparing and contrasting prior learning to current experience

MATERIALS

Clip boards

Pencils/pens

Question/data sheet

PROCEDURES

Prior to leaving on an actual field trip or entering the site of a virtual field trip, students should be prepared for what they will experience. Reducing the novelty effect of the experience will better support student learning (Olson, Cox-Petersen, &

McComas, 2001). If students will be exploring specific questions, it will be important to provide guidance to help students discover this information at the site or appropriately connect to prior classroom learning. If data sheets are being used, the following questions should be considered:

1. Should data be recorded as it is encountered at the field trip site?
2. Will time be given after the trip to complete the data sheet?
3. Are data sheets to be completed individually or as a group?
4. Can adult chaperones assist with data sheet completion?

Chaperones and guides for actual field trips should be told of teachers' expectations for completion of the question/data sheets and for student behavior.

GRADE-LEVEL MODIFICATIONS

K–2nd Grade

Making field trips an important part of the early childhood curriculum is critical. Even the youngest children will find the authentic context of a field trip supports understanding of abstract concepts and engages their natural curiosity (Melber, 2007, 2008b). Identifying personally relevant elements of a field trip will be important for this age range. For example, tying the trip to a theme, such as "where does our food come from," is helpful for these young learners. Chaperones can be asked to talk with their charges and allow children to dictate answers to the data sheet questions. Children may also be asked to draw what they discover.

3rd Grade–5th Grade

Teaching this age of learner how to take notes as they participate on the field trip is important. They should be taught how to transform these notes into answers to the data sheet questions. Some educators find clipboards to be helpful during a field trip (Parker, 2009), yet others may find these to be cumbersome. Choose what works best for you and your students. Ensuring data sheets contain open-ended questions that allow for students to focus on areas of personal interest can provide intrinsic motivation, which can translate into greater cognitive gains (Covington, 1998).

6th Grade–8th Grade

Much of the responsibility for developing questions to be investigated and answered during the real or virtual should be given to this age group. As with all grade levels, creating experiences that parallel the work of social scientists is critical. As a class, have students identify areas related to their curriculum about which they still have questions. These can then be the focus of the field trip experience. Students can be broken into groups around these areas of personal interest to maximize intrinsic motivation for the day's activities, however, teachers of this age level will need to pay particular attention to the final make-up of groups. Sometimes when learners are out of the familiar environment of the school, their behavior might be different. Teachers need to be aware of the dynamics between and among students as they determine groups and also need to have chaperones aware of possible concerns.

MEETING THE NEEDS OF ENGLISH LEARNERS

Field trips are especially helpful for English learners as they provide authentic context that can support learning in a less-pressured environment (Melber, 2008a). To further support these learners, questions on the data sheets should be worded so that they are easily understood and then answered. Providing learners with copies of guides made available by the field trip site can give these learners additional help by connecting vocabulary with images. Sometimes these guides are even available in the primary language of your English learners.

MEETING THE NEEDS OF STUDENTS WITH SPECIAL NEEDS

It is essential that teachers be aware of the accommodations and adaptations that are made at the field trip site to assist learners with disabilities. Is the site wheelchair friendly? How far apart are elements on the site? Are restrooms accessible? Is Braille used on signage? When they visit the sites prior to the class field trip, teachers should be certain that accommodations are those needed by their students. With regard to virtual field trips, teachers should be sure that accommodations using assistive technology can be provided to students who may need additional support.

ASSESSMENT SUGGESTION

At the conclusion of this activity, students will be able to:

- Relate classroom learning to actual or virtual experience
- Answer questions that require them to think critically about the experience
- Work collaboratively to expand personal thinking

Students' answers to the questions on the data sheet can be assessed using the following rubric:

Score	Criteria
4	All answers are complete with exceptional detail and show that the student or group thought critically and related classroom learning and field trip experience.
3	All answers are complete with sufficient detail and show that student or group thought critically.
2	Most of the answers are complete, or some answers do not show critical thinking and connections.
1	Few of the answers are complete, and little or no critical thinking and connections are evident.

Children's Literature Connection

These books begin with basic questions about the place to be visited. Vocabulary is easy so young students can read them for themselves. They can be used to establish procedures and questions for social science related field trips.

Out and About at the Theater

> By Bitsy Kemper
>
> ISBN: 140482281X

This book is part of a series and begins with basic questions about the place to be visited. Vocabulary is easy so young students can read it for themselves. The book can be used as a model to establish procedures and questions for social science related field trips.

Ultimate Field Trip #4: A Week in the 1800s

> By Susan Goodman
>
> ISBN: 0689842600

This book tells a story about a middle-school field trip to a historical settlement. The experiences detailed in this selection can be used by teachers to help prepare their students for real and virtual field trips.

Ultimate Field Trip #2: Digging Into Southwest Archaeology

> By Susan Goodman
>
> ISBN: 0689838913

This book can be used to help learners get ready for real and virtual field trips. The work of current-day archaeologists as well as the Native American culture are presented.

Quick Fact

The virtual field trip site for Colonial Williamsburg has a call-in feature where students can "talk" to historical personages like George Washington.

FIGURE 8.1 "During My Visit . . ." Sample Data Sheet	K–2nd Grade

I saw this:

I learned that . . .

_____

_____

_____

_____

_____

_____

_____

_____

_____

_____

_____

_____

_____

I wonder . . .

_____

_____

_____

_____

_____

_____

_____

_____

_____

_____

_____

_____

_____

_____

_____

REFERENCES

Bamberger, Y., & Tal, T. (2007). Learning in a personal context: Levels of choice in a free choice learning environment in science and natural history museums. *Science Education, 91*(1), 75–95.

Chapin, J. R. (2005). *Elementary social studies: A practical guide.* Boston: Allyn & Bacon.

Covington, M. V. (1998). *The will to learn: A guide for motivating young people.* Cambridge, UK: Cambridge University Press.

Kisiel, J. (2003). Teachers, museums and worksheets: A closer look at a learning experience. *Journal of Science Teacher Education, 14*(1), 3–21.

Melber, L. M. (2007). Maternal scaffolding in two museum exhibition halls. *Curator, 50,* 341–354.

Melber, L. M. (2008a). *Informal learning and field trips: Engaging students in standards based experiences across the K-5 curriculum.* Thousand Oaks, CA: Corwin Press.

Melber, L. M. (2008b). Science museums and the young learner. *Dimensions of Early Childhood Education, 36,* 22–29.

National Council for the Social Studies. (1994). *Expectations of excellence: Curriculum standards for social studies.* Washington, DC: Author.

National Council of Teachers of English and International Reading Association. (1996). *Standards for the English language arts.* Urbana, IL: National Council of Teachers of English.

Olson, J. K., Cox-Petersen, A. M., & McComas, W. F. (2001). The inclusion of informal environments in science teacher preparation. *Journal of Science Teacher Education, 12*(3), 155–173.

Parker, W. C. (2009). *Social studies in elementary education.* Upper Saddle River, NJ: Prentice Hall.

Sunal, C. S., & Haas, M. E. (2005). *Social studies for the elementary and middle grades: A constructivist approach* (2nd ed.). Boston: Allyn & Bacon.

Conducting Social Science Fieldwork

Strategy 9

ARCHITECTURE ANALYSIS

"Our teacher told us today that we were going to be doing a history project," explained Ariel. "At first I was so happy! I wanted to go home and make a poster about our town and the buildings in it."

"That really sounds like stuff we did when we were younger. How boring!" remarked Randy.

"Wait! Then our teacher said I couldn't do the poster without doing research. I am so mad. She wants all of us to be parts of a team that gathers information about our town. Then we put the information together. It's something called being an ethnographer, whatever that is," continued Ariel. "It seems like a lot of extra work!"

"Sounds great to me," countered Randy. "You work in groups to discover something new about where we live."

"Gosh, when you put it that way, it does sound kinda fun. Maybe I'll like the project after all," concluded Ariel.

Teaching elementary students to "do" social science—to be social scientists—provides them the opportunity to construct and compose knowledge that is relevant and important to them and their classmates. This construction of knowledge involves the gathering of data, selection of relevant data, interpretation of this relevant material, and reflection on the process of collection and the subsequent findings. One method is to have students emulate the work of ethnographers, who do extensive fieldwork to collect rich information from which to draw conclusions (Hubbard, 1996). When conducted by students, such fieldwork can involve examining aspects of their classroom, their school, their neighborhood, or their community.

Beginning with their own classrooms, learners can examine the phenomena of what goes on in their classroom. As social scientists, they work in teams to record what is happening. At a specific time and for a specified amount of minutes, each group records what they see. Teachers determine when the entire class will meet to compare and contrast results. Then the class will compile a description of what goes on in their classroom on a typical day. Parker (2009) recommends that students write a "thick" description after such a field study to align with the work done by professional ethnographers. Teachers can then read the journals of Lewis and Clark to their class as historical examples of such rich description. Although the work of a true ethnographer will be significantly more detailed and involved than the classroom example provided here, this is a first step in introducing students to the process of social science research.

Learners can then expand this classroom experience to their school. Parker (2009) suggests that learners as social scientists observe and describe their school cafeteria. Other areas of the school that can be studied include the media center, entrance to the building, and the principal's office. After students collate their results, the writing of the description can be directed to a particular audience. The audience could be students in the school in 2020, a visitor from another country, or any other person or group the teacher and students choose. The addition of an audience requires the class to be sure that all facts are recorded and interpreted clearly and without bias.

Learners can expand the classroom and school experiences to help them learn about their community. They can record such things as observations of what happens at certain times and for specified time intervals in their home or neighborhood. These observations can be extended to include having students gather data about such community aspects as architecture. Once the learners, as social scientists, collect the information and record their observations in an unbiased way, they can be taught to analyze what their data indicate about their community.

Please visit www.sagepub.com/lmelberstudy for the updated National Council of the Social Studies standards.

Curriculum Standards for Social Studies

- Strand I: Culture
- Strand II: Time, Continuity, & Change
- Strand III: People, Places, & Environment
- Strand IV: Individual Development & Identity
- Strand VIII: Science, Technology, & Society

Standards for the English Language Arts

Students will not only be utilizing language arts skills through the completion of data sheets and small group discussion but also through the research they conduct on the different architectural sites.

- Standard 7:   Students conduct research on issues and interests by generating ideas and questions, and by posing problems. They gather, evaluate, and synthesize data from a variety of sources (e.g., print and nonprint texts, artifacts, people) to communicate their discoveries in ways that suit their purpose and audience.

- Standard 8:   Students use a variety of technological and informational resources (e.g., libraries, databases, computer networks, video) to gather and synthesize information and to create and communicate knowledge.

Sources: National Council for the Social Studies, 1994; National Council of Teachers of English and International Reading Association, 1996.

Technology Connection

Students may want to use the Internet to search archives to learn more about architecture styles from different eras. Students should also be reminded of the large role that technology plays in new architectural design work, which is a different approach from the earlier use of smaller scale models.

KEY THEMES

Making observations

Distinguishing between fact and opinion

Hypothesizing

Recording data

MATERIALS

Data chart

Pictures provided by electronic sources

Pictures provided by local historical society or owners of buildings

PROCEDURES

After giving a brief background concerning architecture, teachers will explain to students that they will be functioning as social scientists who will be observing architecture in their own community.

Students should come to understand that architecture is the science and art of designing and creating buildings that are useful and appealing. Architects design individual buildings. A community is composed of many buildings with various purposes, and most times, a community is not planned but rather evolves. Looking at the architecture of the buildings in their community will give learners a glimpse at the history of not only the environment but of the people who created their town.

Teachers should then explain the assignment and procedure to the learners. They will be social scientists doing research similar to the way an ethnographer would. They can study the buildings in their community through a variety of methods. They could walk the community with their teacher and class, divided into pairs or groups to record what they see on a data chart (see Figure 9.1 on p. 68). Recording can be as simple as counting the number of houses, houses of worship, public buildings, or stores seen. When the class returns to school, students can compare their numbers, make a class chart, and then make some conclusions about their community. Recording can be more elaborate as learners can identify specific types of architecture and count them. Cameras can be provided to be used to take relevant pictures so that learners remember what they have seen. However, students need to be instructed about respecting the property of others and privacy issues. For example, before taking pictures of a home, perhaps teachers can contact the homeowner for permission.

If it is not possible or convenient for students to take a walk to do their work as ethnographers, teachers can provide pictures of buildings in the community using electronic sources or by contacting a local historical society or building owners. Students can study these pictures to make observations about the town's prevalent architecture and can make conclusions about the people and environment in the past and the present. Guest speakers from the historical society, the community, or an architectural company can be asked to address the class about what they have observed.

GRADE-LEVEL MODIFICATIONS

K–2nd Grade

This age group should start by collecting data in their classroom or school as a group. Teachers should direct the gathering of information and be sure that learners are counting accurately. To examine architecture of the community, these young students can be asked to bring in pictures of their own homes or houses of worship, and the class can make conclusions as they examine all of the pictures together.

3rd Grade–5th Grade

Emphasis with these students should be on teaching them to record data without making judgments or conclusions. Counting events or architectural styles will be facilitated by the data sheet. Students should be taught to use lines to record and then tally the total. However, as students record their analysis as an individual, group, or whole class, they will need to be cautioned about recording facts and not their personal opinions about the architecture they observed.

6th Grade–8th Grade

Teachers can work with art teachers and technology teachers to have these learners make authentic models of the architecture they have observed. Using these models, students can create a model of their whole community or sections of it. This re-creation can also be done through computer simulations. Creating a physical model can help the class visualize the reasons for certain types of architecture.

MEETING THE NEEDS OF ENGLISH LEARNERS

A word bank or word wall can be provided to help learners understand architectural terms. Students can be encouraged to draw rather than write responses to certain questions on the data sheet.

MEETING THE NEEDS OF STUDENTS WITH SPECIAL NEEDS

If teachers choose to use the walking and observing activity, they need to be certain that the area to be walked is accessible to all. If teachers chose to focus on exploring print images, teachers need to be sure that the pictures are of sufficient size and clarity that all can see. Learners with low vision can benefit from having access to magnifying devices.

ASSESSMENT SUGGESTION

At the conclusion of this activity, students will be able to:

- Distinguish between fact and opinion
- Make careful observations
- Understand the importance of recording accurately
- Comprehend how the architecture of their community depends on the people who constructed the buildings and the geography of the location

Students' data sheets will be assessed using the following rubric:

Score	Criteria
4	All sections of the data sheet are complete, and student has made an effective analysis of what the data indicate.
3	All sections are complete, and student has made an adequate analysis of what the data indicate.
2	Most of the data sections are complete, and student has made some insignificant conclusions.
1	Few of the sections are complete, and student has made some errors in conclusion.

Children's Literature Connection

Architects Make Zigzags
> By Diane Maddex
> ISBN: 047114357X
> This alphabet book provides easy-to-understand definitions accompanied by black-line illustrations of various architectural terms.

The Art of Construction: Projects and Principles for Beginning Engineers and Architects
> By Mario Salvadori
> ISBN: 1556520808
> This very detailed, award-winning book presents architecture as humanity's response to the needs of survival and shelter.

Quick Fact

The use of steel skeletons and frameworks has made it possible to build skyscrapers. The walls of these buildings are not for support but really are used simply to enclose the buildings' frameworks and provide a finished look.

FIGURE 9.1 Examining Architecture Sample Data Sheet   3rd–5th

Count how many houses you see: _____

Count how many places of worship you see: _____

Count how many stores you see: _____

Draw a picture of one of the buildings you have seen.

Why did you pick this building to draw?

_____

_____

_____

Write down three facts about the buildings you have seen.

1. _____

_____

2. _____

_____

3. _____

_____

Talk with your group or class about what you saw, and reach three conclusions about what the buildings in your neighborhood tell us about the people and environment in which you live.

1. _____

_____

2. _____

_____

3. _____

_____

REFERENCES

Hubbard, R. (1996). Young ethnographers: Children conducting case studies in a multiage classroom. *Teaching and Learning, 10*(3), 14–20.

National Council for the Social Studies. (1994). *Expectations of excellence: Curriculum standards for social studies.* Washington, DC: Author.

National Council of Teachers of English and International Reading Association. (1996). *Standards for the English language arts.* Urbana, IL: National Council of Teachers of English.

Parker, W. C. (2009). *Social studies in elementary education.* Upper Saddle River, NJ: Prentice Hall.

Strategy
10

Incorporating
Service Learning

COMMUNITY SERVICE PROJECT

"So Latoya, did you know in our classroom we are trying to help each other out?" bragged Andy.

"No, I didn't know," said Latoya, "Why are you doing that?"

"Our teacher told us that one part of social studies is for us to be better citizens. Mr. Hunter says we can be better citizens by beginning in our own classroom," clarified Andy.

"I bet my class can be good citizens too by helping others in our school, home, and neighborhood, too," replied Latoya.

Service learning is an integral part of preparing students to be citizens who take responsibility for others and contribute to the betterment of society. Specifically, this learning should combine service to others with social studies learning (Soslau & Yost, 2007).

Teachers should strive to structure experiences that involve learners in school-based, community-based, or individual projects. One of the best ways to suggest and organize such experiences is to brainstorm with students what they see as projects in which they want to be involved. They can examine or be prodded to look at issues and opportunities in their homes, schools, community, the nation, and the world.

It is essential that teachers of elementary students consider age- and developmentally appropriate ways for learners to become socially conscious (Terry, 2008). Having students ask their parents for money to support a cause does not require the learners themselves to do anything. Rather, young learners should really be doing something that requires their active participation. The activity can be as simple as creating cards for nursing-home patients or for faculty members who are ill. Service learning projects can become increasingly complex as students get older. In addition, they can participate in helping activities as members of a class group or individually. Service projects also can be planned in advance, such as uniting with an ecological organization to study streams in the area or creating a garden to help relieve hunger, or they can be the spontaneous response to unique situations, such as helping victims of flooding and fires.

Parents and families should be made aware of the parameters of service projects and what is expected of them. Are parents required to drive their students to a location? Are parents asked to assist in such activities such as cleaning up a local park or beach? Parents need to be assured that their children will not be exposed to activities or incidents that are inappropriate, unsuitable, or dangerous. For example, although it is an ideal activity for older elementary students to tutor younger ones, an adult needs to supervise such teaching.

Having learners identify school and community issues and concerns that they can address through service learning asks them to think beyond themselves and display empathy toward others. Students can be asked to brainstorm and list ways that they can help others. Teachers can also monitor whether the suggestions are within the purview of the learners' abilities and responsibilities and guide instruction from there.

Sources: National Council for the Social Studies, 1994; National Council of Teachers of English and International Reading Association, 1996.

Please visit www.sagepub.com/lmelberstudy for the updated National Council of the Social Studies standards.

Curriculum Standards for Social Studies

- Strand IV: Individual Development & Identity
- Strand V: Individuals, Groups, & Institutions
- Stand VI: Power, Authority, & Governance
- Strand X: Civic Ideals & Practice

Standards for the English Language Arts

Students will rely heavily on language arts skills to not only research and frame the problem but to communicate their plan to their peers and the school community.

- Standard 7:   Students conduct research on issues and interests by generating ideas and questions, and by posing problems. They gather, evaluate, and synthesize data from a variety of sources (e.g., print and nonprint texts, artifacts, people) to communicate their discoveries in ways that suit their purpose and audience.

- Standard 8:   Students use a variety of technological and informational resources (e.g., libraries, databases, computer networks, video) to gather and synthesize information and to create and communicate knowledge.

Technology Connection

Suggestions for service projects can be accessed at www.nationalservice.org, which is a site sponsored by the Corporation for National and Community Service. You may also want to tap into friends, colleagues, and family members through social networking sites to create a network of problem solvers around the nation!

KEY THEMES

Identifying problems that can be addressed through service

Recognizing the responsibilities of a citizen

Suggesting solutions for problems that can be answered through service learning

Communicating to others respectfully

MATERIALS

Data sheets

Resources (print, nonprint, human, organizations) that can help learners clarify service learning needs and opportunities

PROCEDURES

Teachers need to guide students to understand their social responsibilities and to comprehend how they can address issues. Beginning with issues in their own classrooms, learners can be challenged to treat each other with respect and caring. "Pretzels" is an activity that has been made popular through the Internet. This activity rewards students for being kind to each other. They are asked to record ways that other learners are helpful and then report them out in a class meeting. Young learners can respond and talk about with such kindnesses as opening the door for each other, sharing materials, and saying please and thank you. Pretzels or other rewards are provided by the teacher for the do-gooders. This activity promotes not only positive interactions but the consideration of others' actions.

Students can be guided through a data sheet to consider concerns in their school, neighborhood, country, and world (see Figure 10.1 on p. 74). They can be asked to consider the needs of younger students and also of senior citizens. They can be asked to think about ways to alert adults to community needs, such as recycling requirements and graffiti clean-up. Most important, learners can be guided to consider ways that they themselves can help address these concerns. They can also be taught to acknowledge the solutions that they cannot implement and to ask others for help.

For some students, it might be necessary to talk and clarify why service learning or community service is important. Values, such as kindness, responsibility, and respect, can be explained and emphasized.

GRADE-LEVEL MODIFICATIONS

K–2nd Grade

Students in this age group need to be helped to understand why they need to care about others. They can complete the data chart as a class and devise ways to help each other learn. These learners can be asked to expand their personal perspective to consider ways they could be polite or help others in the school building. They can write thank-you notes or make thank-you pictures for the school secretary, principal, or janitors. These young learners can also be asked to consider how their family members help them and can then write thank you notes or create pictures for parents, grandparents, brothers, sisters, and caregivers.

3rd Grade–5th Grade

These students can be challenged to identify ways they themselves can be involved in improving their school and community. After they complete their data sheet to identify issues, they can create posters, newspapers, or poems that tell about the problem and the solution.

6th Grade–8th Grade

The activities that students at this age level identify as solutions to problems identified on their data sheets should be further classified according to responsibility and accountability. These learners should be taught to consider ways they as a class, smaller group, or individual can respond. For example, if a student is considered responding as an individual to a concern, the student needs to understand that he or she needs to manage time well and be self-motivated and self-directed.

MEETING THE NEEDS OF ENGLISH LEARNERS

Students who are English learners are often most aware of needs for younger English learners. Some may naturally want to be involved with tutoring these students or creating materials to help them learn better. Others may benefit from working with students who are not English learners and tutoring them in other areas they may excel in. English-language learners can also help their school media specialists select books that they enjoy.

MEETING THE NEED OF STUDENTS WITH DISABILITIES

For this project, it is important that students without disabilities not concentrate on helping students with disabilities as a form of service project. Rather, students without disabilities should be helped to understand that students with disabilities are also students with significant abilities. Students with disabilities should be encouraged by teachers to use their abilities to help others. Students with disabilities should not be forced into an advocacy role, as individuals have varied levels of comfort in this role. For those who are interested in serving in an advocacy role, they may want to focus on promoting a greater understanding of living with a disability among their peers or community.

ASSESSMENT SUGGESTION

At the conclusion of the activity, students will be able to:

- Identify a problem in their classroom, school, community, nation, or the world
- Select a solution that they themselves can implement to alleviate this problem
- Explain why the suggested solution is appropriate

Students' data sheets can be assessed using the following rubric:

Score	Criteria
4	All sections of the data sheet are complete, with exceptional detail and insight.
3	All sections are complete, with an acceptable level of detail.
2	Most of the sections are complete, with an acceptable amount of detail, or all sections completed with errors.
1	Few of the sections are complete, or multiple errors are present.

Children's Literature Connection

The Complete Guide to Service Learning

    By Cathryn Kaye

    ISBN: 157542133X

    This book is based on the premise that it will help guide learners and teachers in ways to connect school curriculum with community experiences.

The Kid's Guide to Service Projects: Over 500 Service Ideas for Young People Who Want to Make a Difference

    By Barbara Lewis and Pamela Espeland

    ISBN: 0915793822

    This is a practical guide suggesting both small- and large-scale projects for young learners to get themselves involved in helping others.

The Kid's Guide to Social Action

    By Barbara Lewis

    ISBN: 1575420384

    This resource provides stories about community involvement as well as reproducible forms for such activities as surveys and grant applications.

Quick Fact

Elementary students can make a difference in their community. Sunal and Haas (2005) report the Extended Learning Program at Jackson Elementary School in Utah has resulted in such community improvements as clean-up of a hazardous waste site, planting of trees, sidewalk improvements, and even passage of two new laws!

FIGURE 10.1	Selecting a Service Learning Project Sample Data Sheet	K–2nd, 3rd–5th, 6th–8th

Topic to be addressed by service project/learning:

_____

_____

_____

_____

Problem identification:

_____

_____

_____

_____

What is the concern?

_____

_____

_____

_____

Why is it a concern?

_____

_____

_____

_____

How did you become aware of this concern?

_____

_____

_____

_____

What are the facts relating to this concern?

_____

_____

_____

_____

Solution/action to be taken:

How will service learning address this concern?

_____

_____

_____

_____

Develop a plan for how service learning can be used to address this concern.

_____

_____

_____

_____

_____

_____

_____

(Continued)

FIGURE 10.1 (Continued)	K–2nd, 3rd–5th, 6th–8th

What specific actions can you take as an individual, as a member of a group, as a member of our class, as part of your family, or as a student at our school?

_____

_____

_____

_____

What could prevent you from being involved in this solution or service learning plan?

_____

_____

_____

_____

How can you overcome this challenge?

_____

_____

_____

_____

REFERENCES

National Council for the Social Studies. (1994). *Expectations of excellence: Curriculum standards for social studies.* Washington, DC: Author.

National Council of Teachers of English and International Reading Association. (1996). *Standards for the English language arts.* Urbana, IL: National Council of Teachers of English.

Soslau, E. G., & Yost, D. S. (2007). Urban service-learning: An authentic teaching strategy to deliver a standards-driven curriculum. *Journal of Experiential Education, 30*(1), 36–53.

Sunal, C. S., & Haas, M. E. (2005). *Social studies for the elementary and middle grades: A constructivist approach* (2nd ed.). Boston: Allyn & Bacon.

Terry, A. (2008). Student voices, global echoes: Service-learning and the gifted. *Roeper Review, 30*(1), 45–51.

UNIT III
Multiple Voices

◆

Current approaches to social studies education acknowledge that there are multiple histories and multiple interpretations of historical events. The importance of this pluralistic approach to social studies curriculum and learning is evident. Such an approach provides students with opportunities to learn beyond facts and figures and to become critical thinkers (Committee on Developments in the Science of Learning, 1999). As critical thinkers, they are involved in investigations and problem solving that encourage them to use multiple sources and interpretations as evidence for their own conclusions. History can and should be studied as an inclusive subject that acknowledges and celebrates the interplay of multiple and diverse viewpoints. Even the youngest elementary students can be challenged to view events from multiple perspectives and perceptions. Encouraging such a pluralistic view of history has the power to provide pupils with the ability to draw their own conclusions. More important, however, is that this encouraging of respect for complexity and diversity has the potential to translate into their appreciating and valuing the differences that make people and all of life so exciting.

Students can be helped to envision multiple images and perspectives through such strategies as comparing artwork, contrasting myths that interpret history, and performing role plays (Duncombe & Heikkinen, 1990) that ask them to imagine other people's lives. They also can be challenged to take a firm stand on an issue so that they are prepared to debate and defend their interpretations and beliefs (Committee on Developments in the Science of Learning, 1999). Finally, museum educators can provide classroom teachers with suggestions for pedagogical techniques that will assist in understanding Native American lifeways (Melber, 2008).

REFERENCES

Committee on Developments in the Science of Learning. (1999). *How people learn: Brain, mind, experience, and school* (J. D. Bransford, A. L. Brown, & R. R. Cockney, Eds.). Washington, DC: National Academies Press.

Duncombe, S., & Heikkinen, M. H. (1990). Role playing for different viewpoints. *Social Studies, 81*(1), 33–35.

Melber, L. M. (2008). *Informal learning and field trips: Engaging students in standards based experiences across the K–5 curriculum.* Thousand Oaks, CA: Corwin Press.

Strategy 11

Connecting With the Visual Arts

VISUAL ARTS ANALYSIS

"Mom, our teacher asked us all to draw pictures of George Washington today," said Josephine. "And do you know what? Everyone's picture looked a little different, and we all drew different parts of his life. I wonder what he really looked like?" she continued.

"Well, I wonder too," her mother remarked. "There are so many portraits and drawings of him and his activities as the father of our country. They are so interesting and tell us so much about him. You've seen the one of him standing in the boat crossing the Delaware River. Do you think this is how he really looked? What do you think he was really doing on that day?"

Teaching young learners to appreciate art as a unique means of communication is indeed a complex task. Social studies teachers can use art to illuminate and to provide multiple perspectives about people or past events. Teachers are challenged to help learners see into the paintings because paintings not only depict subjects and the artist's interpretations but also say much about the time and the place when the art was created (Janson & Janson, 2003).

Students, particularly those who are visual learners, like to look at paintings and learn much by considering what the artist chose to depict. Teachers can simply use art to introduce a lesson and have students brainstorm about what they see and how it might relate to what they are going to study. For example, displaying a copy of Sheeler's "American Scene," which depicts a train and factory could be used to introduce the youngest learners to a unit on transportation and the importance of railroad for shipping goods. Learners can be further challenged to consider how this painting with its rigid block shapes yet realistic portrayal makes them feel. Thus, students can be taught to look into and beyond the subject of the work to consider the total design and artistic elements that make up the composition.

This looking into and beyond the subject can assist them to develop the ability to see that the study of historical events is also subject to interpretation. History, as recorded in words and books and in art and photographs, is dependent on the eye, pen, paint, and perspective of the recorder. Presenting even the youngest learners with a multitude of paintings about the same subject or person will help them better understand key historical events and learn to discuss how different interpretations of history can be portrayed and communicated through the visual arts medium. The presenting of multiple perceptions, literally and figuratively, will allow them to develop their own thoughts and perceptions through comparison and contrast with the thoughts and perceptions of historians and artists.

Finally, teachers of social studies can unite with art teachers to create interdisciplinary units and connections that revolve around social studies topics (Gullatt, 2008). Such teacher interaction and collaboration not only enhances and amplifies student learning but also provides a model of cooperation for students.

Sources: National Council for the Social Studies, 1994; National Council of Teachers of English and International Reading Association, 1996.

Please visit www.sagepub.com/lmelberstudy for the updated National Council of the Social Studies standards.

Curriculum Standards for Social Studies

- Strand II: Time, Continuity, & Change
- Strand III: People, Places, & Environments
- Strand V: Individuals, Groups, & Institutions

Standards for the English Language Arts

In addition to written completion of the data sheet, this activity offers the opportunity for particularly rich discussion which can support development of advanced oral language and communication skills.

- Standard 8:   Students use a variety of technological and informational resources (e.g., libraries, databases, computer networks, video) to gather and synthesize information and to create and communicate knowledge.

- Standard 12:   Students use spoken, written, and visual language to accomplish their own purposes (e.g., for learning, enjoyment, persuasion, and the exchange of information).

Technology Connection

The Internet has a wealth of images to draw from to deliver this activity. Many art museums even have curricula to guide discussions on works of art for the classroom setting. Others may have their collections archived electronically so even if you cannot make it to the museum, you can still explore their collections.

KEY THEMES

Making observations

Analyzing observational data

Comparing and contrasting varying interpretations

Testing hypotheses

Making inferences

Communicating understanding

MATERIALS

Copies of two or three paintings depicting the same or similar subject, person, or time period depending on the social studies unit being studied (Available in art and museum stores as well as on many Internet sites. These Internet displays are ideal because teachers can project them large enough so that everyone can see.)

Two data sheets per student—one about general viewing; the other for comparison and contrast

PROCEDURES

Prior to this particular lesson, depending on the age of the learners and the teachers' intent, teachers will want to provide instruction about how to look at art. Such instruction can be a brief overview of how to look at and appreciate art by not only considering the subject but also by looking at the total design of the work (see Figure 11.1 on p. 83). What is shown in the foreground? What is shown in the background? Why do you think the artist chose to use certain colors or shapes? Some teachers might want to expand their students' understanding by introducing basic art terminology, such as representational, realistic, and abstract art or by discussing formal elements such as line, shape, texture, and space.

For this lesson, students are exposed to two or three works about the same subject. This lesson can take place before studying a time period, unit, or person as an introductory activity, during studying to amplify learning, or after studying to confirm what students know and understand. Learners are asked to complete a data sheet for each artwork and then a comparison and contrast sheet to synthesize their learning (see Figure 11.2 on p. 84). It is essential that teachers model what they expect learners to comprehend and complete. For example, teachers could provide three paintings relating to George Washington—one of Stuart's portraits, Savage's portrayal of the Washington family, and Leutze's painting of the crossing of the Delaware. Teachers should complete one of the data sheets relating to an individual picture with the whole class as a model of what to do. Young students particularly find it fascinating to have the class together examine the painting of the Washington's family. For some, it is the first time they comprehend that the people studied in social studies class are like them, with families and personal lives! For older students, teachers might begin with one of Stuart's portraits and relate the painting to the idea that during the founding of the nation, there were some who wanted to portray Washington as perfect leader, king, or god so that people would unite under his leadership to form a stable United States.

After modeling, teachers need to provide ample time for students to study the paintings and to answer the questions. Learners can work individually, in pairs, or in groups to complete all data sheets. At all grade levels, it is interesting to pair students for this activity. Each member of the pair can provide insight though what he or she sees, and the pair can then produce a collaborative data sheet in which they display their ability to not only comprehend but also to analyze and synthesize each other's thoughts.

GRADE-LEVEL MODIFICATIONS

K–2nd Grade

Usually young students in social studies will be learning about things and places near them, such as their school, community, or state. These students can be provided with artwork that depicts their local community or shows people they are familiar with as they work, such as doctors, nurses, dentists, and law enforcement officers. Providing artwork showing the local community can lead to a comparison and contrast discussion of how a location has changed over time, which helps these learners understand the concepts of time and change. Providing artwork showing examples of people at work can lead to a comparison of, for example, how their own "real" doctor compares with the one in the painting. Norman Rockwell's paintings of real-life situations work well with this age level.

3rd Grade–5th Grade

At this age level, students can work without too much teacher assistance to complete the data sheets. They can use the comparison and contrast data sheet as a prewrite for an essay in which they develop a thesis or main idea either about the event or person depicted or about why the artists chose to create as they did. Also, teachers can consider having these students create their own portraits or paintings to depict what they are studying throughout the school year. This project would be an ongoing venture that could be turned into and displayed as a graphic timeline of what was studied during the entire school year.

6th Grade–8th Grade

Learners can be challenged not only to complete an essay based on the results of their data sheet information, comparisons, and contrasts, but also to find another picture (either a painting or a photograph) depicting the same subject. They can then incorporate this picture into their essay or simply complete an additional comparison and contrast data sheet including what they discovered. Students also would find it fun to create living tableaus by dressing up and posing as some of the paintings.

MEETING THE NEEDS OF ENGLISH LEARNERS

Sometimes the oral ability of English learners is more developed than their written ability. They could give their responses orally, and a scribe could be assigned to help these learners complete the data sheets. Data sheets could also be reconstructed to include only questions that require one-word, yes/no, or true/false answers.

MEETING THE NEEDS OF STUDENTS WITH SPECIAL NEEDS

This activity emphasizes both visual acuity and written communication. Teachers need to be sure that students who need assistance in viewing the paintings have access to text enlargement software that provides the ability to control magnification and contrast. With regard to written communication, providing students with outlining and webbing software, such as Inspiration, gives students who have difficulty with written communication help in recording and organizing their thoughts.

Assessment Suggestion

At the conclusion of this activity, students will be able to:

• Examine artwork for content and form
• Relate artwork to its historical subject and time period
• Compare and contrast artwork depicting the same subject, time period, or event

Students' data sheets will be assessed using the following rubric:

Score	Criteria
4	All sections of the data sheet are complete, and student has made an effective analysis of what the data indicate.
3	All sections are complete, and student has made an adequate analysis of what the data indicate.
2	Most of the data sections are complete, and student has made some insignificant conclusions.
1	Few of the sections are complete, and student has made some errors in conclusion.

Children's Literature Connection

Art Is
> By Bob Raczka
> ISBN: 978–0761318323
>
> This book for young elementary students introduces art from various time periods. The text is in the form of rhyming couplets that amuse and delight young students.

Art Up Close
> By Claire d'Harcourt
> ISBN: 978–0811854641
>
> A range of artwork from different time periods, cultures, and mediums are represented in this visually appealing volume.

Cave Paintings to Picasso: The Inside Scoop on 50 Art Masterpieces
> By Henry Sayre
> ISBN: 978–08118376675
>
> The social and historical context as well as the reasons for painting of each work are detailed. Fifty major works of art from 22,000 B.C. to 1964 are featured.

Usborne: The Children's Book of Art
> By Rosie Dickins
> ISBN: 978–0794512231
>
> The book provides general information about art with details about various types of art (splatter art, etc.) and specific works of art (*The Milkmaid*, etc.). Internet links expand the book's contents.

Quick Fact

Gilbert Stuart, who painted many portraits of George Washington, reported that the father of our country was sometimes difficult to paint. The artist claimed the he had a hard time getting Washington to "look natural." Stuart engaged Washington in talking about horses and farming to try to get him to relax.

FIGURE 11.1	Looking Closely at Paintings Sample Data Sheet	3rd–5th, 6th–8th

Name _____

Title of painting _____

What do you see in this painting?

_____

_____

_____

_____

What do you see in the foreground?

_____

_____

_____

_____

What do you see in the background?

_____

_____

_____

_____

Why do you think the artist chose this approach for his or her painting?

_____

_____

_____

_____

FIGURE 11.2 Comparing Works of Art Sample Data Sheet   3rd–5th, 6th–8th

What historical event, person, or time is depicted in the paintings?

_____

_____

_____

_____

How are the paintings alike? Comment on the subject of the paintings as well as their style.

_____

_____

_____

_____

How are the paintings different from each other?

_____

_____

_____

_____

Why do you think each of the artists chose to show the subject in the style they did?

_____

_____

_____

_____

What did you learn from your analysis about the time period, event, or person depicted in these paintings?

_____

_____

_____

_____

REFERENCES

Gullatt, D. E. (2008). Enhancing student learning through arts integration: Implications for the profession. *The High School Journal, 91*(4), 12–26.

Janson, H. W., & Janson, A. F. (2003). *History of art* (6th ed., Rev.). Upper Saddle River, NJ: Pearson/ Prentice Hall.

National Council for the Social Studies. (1994). *Expectations of excellence: Curriculum standards for social studies.* Washington, DC: Author.

National Council of Teachers of English and International Reading Association. (1996). *Standards for the English language arts.* Urbana, IL: National Council of Teachers of English.

Culturally Responsive Teaching Techniques

Strategy 12

NATIVE AMERICAN RESOURCE EXPLORATION

"I think I know what this could have been used for!" shouted Ashley as she carefully stroked a swatch of bison hide. "The bison provided meat, and leather, and a bunch of other resources Native Americans living in the Central Plains could have used!"

"You're right," answered Mr. Washington. "Can you find another natural resource that could go along with the bison hide?"

"The grass!" answered Kwame. "If there wasn't any grass, there wouldn't be anything for the bison to eat!"

"Yes! I think we're learning there are a lot of ways that natural resources influenced the lifeways of Native Americans," responded Mr. Washington.

❖

Learning about the history and cultural traditions of Native Americans is a prominent element of the K through 8th-grade curriculum in most states. However, although a prominent topic, it is also one that many educators struggle to share with accuracy and cultural respect. Like many concepts in the social studies, activities that were once popular no longer align with our current understanding of cultural understanding and a pluralistic view of history.

Sometimes there is confusion about the language we use when discussing Native American culture. The terms *Native American* or *American Indian* are both respectful choices, but to better acknowledge the diversity of culture in the Native community, using a specific tribal name is preferred (National Museum of the American Indian, 2004; Natural History Museum of Los Angeles County, 2003). Referring to tribes specifically and exploring traditions in detail can help students avoid generalizations and stereotypes. Student knowledge of Native American culture is often limited to what they have encountered in the media (National Museum of the American Indian, 2004) and may be inaccurately centered on tipis and feathered adornments. Your classroom is a great opportunity to share the rich diversity that is the core of Native American culture (Field Museum Education Department, 2007) and work to dispel these misconceptions. It is important to recognize that you may have some students with Native American ancestry and be sensitive to this fact as you design your instruction. However, it's important not to single out these students as information sources, as they may be shy speaking in front of the class or may have limited knowledge of their Native American heritage (Field Museum Education Department, 2007). Providing opportunities for all students to share traditions and information about their ancestry as they choose is a more appropriate option.

There are a number of careful considerations to make when planning Native American–themed activities. In general, it is best to exercise special sensitivity when exploring themes of spirituality or ceremony (Field Museum Education Department, 2007). The act of simplifying these concepts to be pedagogically appropriate for young children can reduce or trivialize these complex concepts in a way that may be considered offensive. These concepts are best treated through group discussion or other methods inclusive of multiple voices to retain their complexity.

Interpretation of culture is by its nature an area of multiple perspectives and varied pedagogical approaches. It is important to recognize that with regard to history and traditions of Native American culture, different opinions can be found among researchers as well as within the Native American community itself, not unlike other areas of cultural study. As you move forward with this activity, as well as any others that center on cultural interpretation, remaining sensitive to the pluralistic nature of cultural interpretation should be at the center of the instructional plan for the best possible result.

Please visit www.sagepub.com/lmelberstudy for the updated National Council of the Social Studies standards.

Curriculum Standards for Social Studies

- Strand I: Culture
- Strand II: Time, Continuity, & Change
- Strand III: People, Places, & Environment

Standards for the English Language Arts

As students discuss their findings they are building oral language skills. Completion of their data sheet provides the opportunity to capture discussion into a written format.

- Standard 4:   Students adjust their use of spoken, written, and visual language (e.g., conventions, style, vocabulary) to communicate effectively with a variety of audiences and for different purposes.

- Standard 5:   Students employ a wide range of strategies as they write and use different writing process elements appropriately to communicate with different audiences for a variety of purposes.

Technology Connection

Many museums now have images and information on artifacts in their collections captured in rich databases. Support students in browsing some of these resources to learn more about Native American artwork, ceremonial artifacts, as well as images and documents.

Sources: National Council for the Social Studies, 1994; National Council of Teachers of English and International Reading Association, 1996.

The Southwest Museum of the American Indian, part of The Autry National Center, is one database you may find helpful. Visit it at http://www.autrynationalcenter.org/southwest/.

Because it can be difficult to know if a lesson or activity is both accurate and a respectful method of interpretation, it is important to identify educator resources that were created by or in consultation with members of Native American communities. Making contact with members of a particular Nation in your community is one way to learn more about cultural traditions. Materials created by anthropological research institutions such as museums can be another helpful source. Examples include:

- Natural History Museum of Los Angeles County. (2003). *Native American curriculum guide.* Available from http://www.nhm.org/education/teachers/NHMNtvAmGd.pdf

- National Museum of the American Indian. (2004). *Print resources.* Available from http://www.nmai.si.edu/subpage.cfm?subpage=education&second=pub

KEY THEMES

Making careful observations

Analyzing observational data

MATERIALS

Data sheets (provided)

Pencils/pens

Colored pencils/crayons

Examples of natural resources, such as water, grass, fur, feathers, and so forth

PROCEDURES

In line with experts' recommendation to focus on tribal specifics whenever possible, this strategy is not structured around exploring generalities. Because there are more then 500 Native American Nations (Field Museum Education Department, 2007) specifying activities for each is well beyond the scope of this work. However, this strategy will be presented as a template for you to use with information specific to the Native American group at the center of your curriculum.

Start by identifying a specific Native American group for the focus on your lesson (see the box on p. 88 for a resource suggestion). Some teachers have district guidelines on focusing on Native American groups that lived and may continue to live locally. Other guidelines may encourage you to explore tribes from different areas of the country. Once you have identified your focus, spend some time researching specific traditions of this group. There are a number of resources available through museums, universities, and other reputable locations to help you gather background information. Many tribes continue a modern and vibrant presence and might be willing to provide background information directly or may even direct you to an informational Web site.

> ## Learning More . . .
>
> This book is an especially helpful and respected resource for educators.
> *Atlas of the North American Indian* (2009)
>   By Carl Waldman
>   ISBN: 0816068585

Through reviewing this background information, identify the many different natural resources that this group used. Gather examples of as many as possible, using photos or other representations of things that may be difficult to procure. Ask students to brainstorm how the different types of natural resources might have been a part of daily life for members of the tribe (see Figure 12.1 on p. 90). For example, all humans need fresh drinking water. Members of the Zuni nation also relied on water as an important part of agriculture. Students may look at a picture of a deer and correctly identify that the meat, hide, and antlers could all be used.

Provide students with the opportunity to share their thoughts with other members of the class. Through group brainstorming, it will soon become apparent that one group likely had many resources. Further exploration might lead to the discovery that different groups might have used some resources in similar ways and some resources quite differently.

GRADE-LEVEL MODIFICATIONS

K–2nd Grade

Students are likely to be concrete in their analysis at this age. Providing resource examples that are familiar to students and easily interpreted is important for this group. Rather than have students complete a data sheet, the activity can be handled as a group discussion with students sitting in a circle on the class rug.

3rd Grade–5th Grade

Students at this grade level can conceptualize one resource having many uses. They will also enjoy respectfully comparing and contrasting how they might use the same resource in their own lives. Provide opportunities for both concrete and abstract connections to build students' analytical skills.

6th Grade–8th Grade

Students at these grade levels might want to explore economic value of different resources. Some resources may have had everyday uses, whereas others were reserved for special occasions or ceremonies. Tribes living in close proximity to each other may have competed for particularly useful or limited resources. Encourage students to explore the availability of each resource and how this might affect its use by a tribe.

MEETING THE NEEDS OF ENGLISH LEARNERS

The use of objects will support English learners by providing authentic context to the discussion. Respectfully exploring diverse cultures in the classroom reinforces to students who may consider themselves different from other students the value of all perspectives, backgrounds, and cultures.

MEETING THE NEEDS OF STUDENTS WITH SPECIAL NEEDS

Sometimes students with learning disabilities can have difficulty understanding abstract concepts. Using actual natural resources provides context that will help with comprehension. Selecting objects that are large and durable will be important for students with limited motor skills. Encouraging students to smell and touch these items will be especially helpful for students with low vision.

ASSESSMENT SUGGESTION

At the conclusion of the activity, students will be able to:

- Carefully illustrate a natural resource
- Make inferences as to how that resource may have been useful
- Support their inferences with factual information

Students' data sheets can be assessed using a simple rubric such as the following:

Score	Criteria
4	All four sections of the data sheet are completed with exceptional detail and insight.
3	Three of the four sections are completed.
2	Two of the four sections are completed.
1	One section is completed, or no work was done.

Children's Literature Connection

It can be difficult to locate literature selections that highlight Native American culture and tradition with the necessary respect and accuracy. Because this can be such a challenge, rather than including a single title here, we've included two Web sites that can help you critically analyze selections and make the best choice for you and your students.

The following site provides information to support you in making informed choices about the inclusion of specific titles related to Native American culture, history, and tradition: "American Indians in Children's Literature" blog: http://americanindiansinchildrensliterature.blogspot.com/.

Created by the Native organization Oyate, this site provides first-voice stories regarding the effect poorly chosen literature can have on children as well as provides helpful lists of positive titles and titles that may be hurtful or offensive: http://www.oyate.org/aboutus.html.

Choosing Language Carefully

Sometimes terms, sayings, and images are so common, we may not immediately recognize them as offensive to individuals and cultural groups (National Museum of the American Indian, 2004). Choose words carefully to avoid using sayings that are derogatory to Native American cultures. Recognize images such as school mascots or retail advertisements that may portray stereotypical images of Native Americans, and ensure they are not a part of your instruction unless it is to specifically explore their inappropriateness.

Quick Fact

Did you know that some of your favorite foods may have Native American origins? The first archaeological evidence of popcorn was found in a cave in New Mexico, dating back more than 5,000 years! Chocolate was first made by the ancient cultures of Mexico and Central America. Although George Washington Carver is thought of as the father of peanut butter and the peanut industry, peanuts had been cultivated by the ancient peoples of South America for thousands of years before he came on the scene. And Thanksgiving just wouldn't be the same without pumpkin pie, right? But Native Americans were cultivating, eating, and using pumpkins long before the first Europeans set foot in America!

FIGURE 12.1   Resource Use Sample Data Sheet   3rd–5th

Natural resource: _____

What are three ways you think this resource was used by the [insert tribal name here]?

1. _____

_____

2. _____

_____

3. _____

_____

Select one of these uses to illustrate below:

What helped you to draw these conclusions?

_____

_____

_____

_____

REFERENCES

Field Museum Education Department. (2007). *The ancient Americas.* Chicago: Field Museum.

National Council for the Social Studies. (1994). *Expectations of excellence: Curriculum standards for social studies.* Washington, DC: Author.

National Council of Teachers of English and International Reading Association. (1996). *Standards for the English language arts.* Urbana, IL: National Council of Teachers of English.

Natural History Museum of Los Angeles County. (2003). *Native American curriculum guide.* Los Angeles: Author.

National Museum of the American Indian. (2004) *A pre-visit guide for teachers.* Washington, DC: Author.

Strategy 13

Connecting With Literature

CREATION MYTH ANALYSIS

"My grandfather told me yesterday that there are many different stories about how the world was created. He told me that his father, who is Native American, told him a story about the start of the world. He talked about the Creator Awonawilona, Earth Mother, and Sun Father," shared John.

As students are challenged to read multiple texts and primary and secondary sources, they can come to see that social studies, particularly history, is not just a collection of facts, events, and dates. Their interpretations and view of history can be further expanded by exposing even the youngest learners to myths and legends. The oral tradition of this type of literature can provide a natural inroad to learning for those who cannot yet read or have difficulty doing so. Teachers can themselves tell the stories, can use recordings, or can even invite a professional storyteller into their classrooms. Students can come to view myths as the essential story of the beginning of human history. These myths and stories from the past, particularly from the time before humans were writing, have survived as ways various cultures explained historical events and occurrences. Finding the commonalities and dissimilarities between different myths can lead students to an appreciation of how humans and cultures are alike and different.

Many myths essentially are stories that a culture or people created long ago to explain the world around them. Natural events such as thunder and rain have spurred many tales. The meaning of human emotions, such as love and hate, also resulted in stories to explain the origin and intent of such feelings. Campbell (1988) reminds us that myths are essential and powerful reading for everyone. He believes that reading and understanding myths provide people with an appreciation of the universe, confirm and validate social order and culture, and teach individuals how to live with and interact meaningfully to each other.

Myths are used by social science researchers to learn more about different societies and cultures. This analysis can assist researchers in learning about values and belief systems of a society as well as the natural wildlife living in proximity with that community. The following activity is a first step to understanding this in-depth research process.

Sources: National Council for the Social Studies, 1994; National Council of Teachers of English and International Reading Association, 1996.

Curriculum Standards for Social Studies

- Strand I: Culture
- Strand II: Time, Continuity, & Change
- Strand V: Individuals, Groups, & Institutions
- Strand IX: Global Connections

Please visit www.sagepub.com/lmelberstudy for the updated National Council of the Social Studies standards.

Standards for the English Language Arts

Students can practice their analytical skills as they explore children's literature and share their thoughts both through discussion and the completion of the Venn Diagram.

- Standard 3:   Students apply a wide range of strategies to comprehend, interpret, evaluate, and appreciate texts. They draw on their prior experience, their interactions with other readers and writers, their knowledge of word meaning and of other texts, their word identification strategies, and their understanding of textual features (e.g., sound–letter correspondence, sentence structure, context, graphics).

- Standard 7:   Students conduct research on issues and interests by generating ideas and questions, and by posing problems. They gather, evaluate, and synthesize data from a variety of sources (e.g., print and nonprint texts, artifacts, people) to communicate their discoveries in ways that suit their purpose and audience.

- Standard 11:   Students participate as knowledgeable, reflective, creative, and critical members of a variety of literacy communities.

- Standard 12:   Students use spoken, written, and visual language to accomplish their own purposes (e.g., for learning, enjoyment, persuasion, and the exchange of information).

Technology Connection

For many people, the differences between myths, legends, and folklore can be difficult to understand and even more challenging to articulate to young people. Kevin Edgecombe (2006) provides a detailed explanation of how these literary works are similar as well as key differences between them in http://www.bombaxo.com/blog/2006/02/myth-legend-folklore.html.

KEY THEMES

Identifying important components of each myth

Describing how the myth solved a problem or explained something for the people who created it

Comparing and contrasting characteristics of myths in general and creation myths in particular

MATERIALS

Copies of myths that are age- and reading-level appropriate (This might require that teachers rewrite myths for their grade level.)

Recordings of myths

Chart paper

Markers

PROCEDURES

This activity requires learners to create a class data chart that can be used to compare and contrast the content of various creation myths. Each student will be given either a written copy or a recording or both of a myth. Each will be responsible for a different story.

Teachers can introduce the activity by defining the word *myth* and explaining the historical roots and significance of this type of story. Reading to the whole class a short poem that contains a myth, such as "Song of Creation"—a poem of the Pima culture—can serve as an easy and accessible way for even the youngest of learners to consider the content and power of myths.

Next, give each student a copy of a different myth. They read or listen to it and then record their findings on the class data chart. Teachers can provide question sheets that will guide students' reading, or learners can use the categories on the data chart for reference. In this jigsaw cooperative learning manner, students are exposed to many different myths. They can be led through class discussion to examine what they and others have placed on the chart and, through this examination, to make comparisons and contrast across myths, people, and cultures.

Teachers can determine or they can work with students to determine what categories to use for the class data chart. Charts for the youngest students could be simplified to include the title and place of origin of the myth and then provide space for them to either draw or write about the main character or event. Older learners can be asked also to record the title and place of origin of the myth, but they should be required to give more details. Descriptions of setting, main characters, other characters, conflicts, and resolutions are appropriate.

A class Venn diagram can be constructed prior to, during, or after all entries are made and discussed. The creation of this visual representation will promote both whole-class and individual analysis and synthesis. Also, the class can make a world map or mark on a commercially prepared map where the countries and regions that fostered the creation myths they read and studied are.

┌───┐

Special Considerations

For some students, stories of creation can have a strong tie to personal religious beliefs. Use your best judgment guided by school policy in conducting this activity to retain the rich experience of exploring different cultures without leading to analysis or exploitation of students' personal belief systems. It is also helpful to assume that any belief system could be shared by a student or students' family members and structure discussion accordingly.

└───┘

GRADE-LEVEL MODIFICATIONS

K–2nd Grade

This age group can work in pairs or as a whole class to complete a simple comparison and contrast data chart. Teachers should spend ample time explaining what the chart will tell the class about different cultures and myths. As an extension of this activity and to help them remember the different stories, students can dress up and pantomime the myths.

3rd Grade–5th Grade

Students can be asked to write their own creation myths based on what they discovered by studying the answers listed on the data chart and contained on the Venn diagram. Their myths would be assessed based on whether their tales contained the essential characteristics of every creation myth and on what creative and original elements were added.

6th Grade–8th Grade

The data chart and the Venn diagram can be used as prewriting strategies for a composition in which students detail various creation myths and their similarities and differences. The composition could be a group effort in which a small number of students contribute summaries and opinions on the particular myth they read and then created a communal thesis and beginning and concluding paragraphs. In addition, students can be challenged to read not only myths but also legends and folklore (see Technology Connections box). They can create data charts and Venn diagrams for these genres also. Then they use all three data charts to make conclusions about how these types of literature are alike and different.

MEETING THE NEEDS OF ENGLISH LEARNERS

Texts and recordings in the language of the learner can be provided. Students, if they are comfortable with this, can share the creation stories of their culture if they know them. They can draw pictures to retell a creation story instead of or in addition to completing the data chart.

MEETING THE NEEDS OF STUDENTS WITH SPECIAL NEEDS

Students who might have difficulty with writing on the class chart could have the chart created on a Smart Board and then transported to their own computers. They could write using their own keyboards, and this would be transmitted to the class chart on the Smart Board. Some learners who have difficulty with reading can use advanced reading aides like Kurzweil Readers. These devices are like talking word processors, but they also guide student reading through such strategies as explaining the definitions of difficult words.

ASSESSMENT SUGGESTION

At the conclusion of this activity, students will be able to:

- Define the characteristics of a myth in general and a creation myth in particular
- Understand the importance of reading thoroughly, accurately, and precisely
- Analyze a work of literature for its components
- Synthesize ideas from various myths

Students' entries on the class data chart can be assessed using the following rubric:

Score	Criteria
4	All categories are filled in completely and accurately.
3	Categories are filled in accurately but not completely.
2	Information is either inaccurate or incomplete.
1	Information is inaccurate and incomplete.

Children's Literature Connection

The Silver Treasure: Myths and Legends of the World
    By Geraldine McCaughrean
    ISBN: 978–0689813221

    Students from third grade and up will be fascinated with this collection. Tales were selected to particularly appeal to and entice this age level.

Reference Book for Teachers

Myths and Hero Tales: A Cross-Cultural Guide to Literature for Children and Young Adults
    By Alethea Helbig and Agnes Perkins
    ISBN: 978–0313299353

    This sourcebook for teachers provides annotated entries regarding 189 books that relate to 1,455 myths and heroes.

In the Beginning: Creation Stories From Around the World
    By Virginia Hamilton
    ISBN: 0152387420

    This book not only contains creation myths, but the author also comments on their origins and provides some interpretation for each entry.

REFERENCES

Campbell, J. (1988). *The power of myth*. New York: Doubleday.

Edgecomb, K. P. (2006, February 10). *Myth, legend, and folklore*. Retrieved May 19, 2009, from http://www.bombaxo.com/blog/2006/02/myth-legend-folklore.html

National Council for the Social Studies. (1994). *Expectations of excellence: Curriculum standards for social studies*. Washington, DC: Author.

National Council of Teachers of English and International Reading Association. (1996). *Standards for the English language arts*. Urbana, IL: National Council of Teachers of English.

Strategy 14

Authentic Role Play

TRAVELING BOX

"I am really sad. We are going to move to Chicago, and my mom said I can't take all of my toys with me. I don't know how to decide. She said I can only take one box full. How can I leave any of my dolls, play ponies, and pet stuff? How can I leave them? I love them all so much!" lamented Rosa.

Rosa's dilemma, as described in the previous vignette, in which she is forced to choose among her most cherished possessions—her toys—echoes in a minor way decisions travelers throughout time have had to make when they decide to go from one place to another. Of course, the decisions made by those who chose to immigrate to new lands or who were forced to leave their own countries were much more monumental than deciding which toys to abandon. These immigrant travelers must first decide where they are going and how will they get there. Questions and dilemmas abound. How will they get the money for their voyage? Will they be accepted once they arrive at their destination? How will they earn a living in this new place? Will the whole family go at the same time? What items that they already own should they bring with them? Should they bring articles that will remind them of their home country? Should they bring items that they know they will need in their new home?

Challenging social studies students to create their own traveling boxes as if they were going on a long journey can assist them in understanding the dilemmas of immigrants and travelers throughout the ages. It can help them realize that students their own age were actually involved in traveling along the Oregon Trail and arriving in the New World on the Mayflower. Creating traveling boxes the size of a shoebox also can help young learners consider what is important to them and their lives. What material possessions—Xbox, PlayStation, and so forth—do they really need to survive and be happy? What is really important to them and their families?

Asking learners to create traveling boxes is also a form of role playing. Most young students love to pretend and go on adventures. Furthermore, Sunal and Haas (2005) posit that role playing can assist students in becoming conscious of their values and beliefs. In creating their traveling boxes, students confront, consciously or subconsciously, some important issues and examine their values. They begin by pretending that they are traveling a long distance and are limited in what they can bring with them. Do they bring essentials like toothpaste and soap? Do they let their parents worry about packing these items? Do they bring their favorite toys and books? Do they take photographs with them? This activity asks teachers to instruct learners about decision making, responsibility, and consequences. For example, if a student decides to cram his or her box full of candy, what is he or she leaving behind? Might he or she get tired of eating only candy? What might be needed at the new destination? How would the student feel if the parents decided only to pack in their boxes things for themselves and not for their children or the family?

Sources: National Council for the Social Studies, 1994; National Council of Teachers of English and International Reading Association, 1996.

Curriculum Standards for Social Studies

- Strand I: Culture
- Strand IV: Individual Development & Identity
- Strand V: Individuals, Groups, & Institutions

Standards for the English Language Arts

Students will have the opportunity to conduct research for this activity using print media as well as orally share their project with their peers.

- Standard 8:   Students use a variety of technological and informational resources (e.g., libraries, databases, computer networks, video) to gather and synthesize information and to create and communicate knowledge.

- Standard 11: Students participate as knowledgeable, reflective, creative, and critical members of a variety of literacy communities.

- Standard 12: Students use spoken, written, and visual language to accomplish their own purposes (e.g., for learning, enjoyment, persuasion, and the exchange of information).

Technology Connection

The Internet can be a great place to find replicas of historic documents for inclusion in an object box focused on a particular time period.

Please visit www.sagepub.com/lmelberstudy for the updated National Council of the Social Studies standards.

KEY THEMES

Generating hypotheses

Solving problems based on understanding actions, responsibilities, and consequences

Making decisions based on data

Thinking critically about one's beliefs and values

MATERIALS

Preliminary class or individual lists

Shoeboxes

Items from home or school selected by individual students (Teachers might want to send home an announcement about this activity to inform parents that students might be bringing to school some unexpected things from home. Parents should be told that items will be returned when the project is finished.)

PROCEDURES

Teachers can begin this activity in a variety of ways. They can couch the introduction in the historical contexts of the various immigrant groups throughout time who have traveled. They can discuss reasons for immigration in the past and present and consider why immigration might happen in the future. Teachers can also begin the activity by discussing the travails of moving, no matter what the time period or how short the distance, as a way to get young learners to relate to the topic. They can talk about what they themselves consider their most prized possession and ask what students value the most.

Next, the idea of collecting items in the space of a shoebox can be introduced. The articles in this box are the only things that students can take on a long voyage. Students can be asked to brainstorm as a class or individually prepare a list of these things. Chick (2008) provides an excellent example of such a list in *Teaching Women's History Through Literature*. However, her list related to what an eight-year-old would bring to America in 1856 (p. 16). After making the class list or individual list, learners should put what they consider the most important in rank order and also consider how many of these items will fit in their shoebox.

Then students should collect the items in the shoebox. Students should be asked either orally or in writing to display their item, explain why they chose what they did, and reflect on whether their decisions were wise ones. Learners can decorate the outside of their boxes in ways reminiscent of the immigrant trunks used by those who came to America in the early 1900s. Teachers can then ask learners why they chose to decorate their boxes as they did. Does the decoration show personality, dreams, destination, or anything else?

GRADE-LEVEL MODIFICATIONS

K–2nd Grade

Teachers can help this age group to make traveling boxes as a whole class or group within the class. An interesting take-off on the traveling box idea that is most relevant for young students is to have them create a "me" box. In the "me" box, they collect different items that they want to share with their next year's teacher. This will give their new teacher an idea of who they are and also help these youngsters remember what work was done and their successes. Pictures, artwork, papers, toys, and so on can be collected in boxes at the end of the school year by each student. They can take these boxes home over the summer and return with them as a first project for the new grade (this is always risky, as things get lost over the summer), or they can create the boxes at the end of the year and show them to the next grade's teachers at that time.

3rd Grade–5th Grade

At this age group, the traveling box activity can be expanded to have students create a traveling box not only for their own time period but also for another time period in the past that they have studied. In addition, they can assume a different persona, such as by creating a box as a president in the 2000s and a president in the 1800s. In these boxes, they could collect pictures, copies of legislation, maps, newspaper articles, and so forth depicting what that person thinks is most significant about his or her time period and presidency. Whether the students create a box about themselves or some other person, it is most important that the emphasis at this age level be on considering, explaining, and reflecting on the reasons for their choices.

6th Grade–8th Grade

Emphasis should be on having students explain either orally or in writing the reasons for their choices. This activity can be expanded to have a class, a group, or an individual create a "culture" box. In this box, students place items that they consider representative of the United States today or of their own lives today. If the activity is done in small groups, they each present their box, and when all are completed, students comment on the similarities and differences noted. Also, the contents of these culture boxes can be shared in a virtual way over the Internet with schools and students of the same age in other countries. They, too, could be asked to create a culture box relating to their country. Students share across the Internet and might be very surprised to find their similarities—particularly in the music they listen to and the clothes they wear.

MEETING THE NEEDS OF ENGLISH LEARNERS

It is particularly important that teachers be sensitive to the fact that some of their students might have been in the exact situation of having to leave their country with little or no warning or possessions. The shoebox activity should be used with care and sensitivity. One modification may be to allow students to select and collect items or pictures of the things that surprised them when they came to the new country, state, or city as an alternative activity.

MEETING THE NEEDS OF STUDENTS WITH SPECIAL NEEDS

This activity is accessible and fun for most students because it revolves around themselves and their own thoughts and decisions. Limiting the number of choices of items or providing a list of suggested items are two activity modifications that may be helpful. For the reflection part of the activity, students who have difficulty writing can record their thoughts electronically.

ASSESSMENT SUGGESTION

At the conclusion of this activity, students will be able to:

- Discuss reasons for their choices
- Determine whether their choices were appropriate
- Examine and determine the differences between needs and wants

Students' shoeboxes and traveling boxes and reflections can be assessed using the following rubric:

Score	Content Criteria	Reflection Criteria
4	Shoebox contained four or more items. Each item was unique.	Student explained clearly and logically why these items were important to him or her either in relation to the student's home or to where he or she was going. At least one item related to where the student was going.
3	Shoebox contain four or more items. Some items were similar to each other.	Student explained in an acceptable manner why items were important. At least one item related to where the student was going.
2	Shoebox contain a few items. Items were similar to each other.	Student had some difficulty explaining why items were important. No items related to where student was going.
1	Items in shoebox were minimal.	Student showed items but could not explain why they were needed.

Children's Literature Connection

Miss Bridie Chose a Shovel

By Leslie Connor

ISBN: 0618305645

This picture book tells the story of all the things that Miss Bridie did with the shovel she brought with her to America when she came in 1856.

How My Family Lives in America

By Susan Kuklin-Bradbury

ISBN: 002751239

This book, written for very young students, tells the true story of three children who immigrated to the United States. Many photos help learners relate to the experiences of the children and families who were originally from Senegal, Puerto Rico, and Taiwan.

Quilted Landscapes: Conversations With Young Immigrants

By Yale Strom

ISBN: 0689800746

The stories of 26 young immigrants are told in this book written for older students. Challenges relating to language acquisition and cultural barriers are well explained.

Quick Fact

Three similar words that refer to moving from one place to another are sometimes are confused by even the most educated individuals. *Emigration* refers to departing from one country or area. *Immigration* refers to entering into a country or area. *Migration* refers to a whole group of people or a whole community moving from one place to another.

REFERENCES

Chick, K. C. (2008). *Teaching women's history through literature: Standards-based lesson plans for grades K–12*. Silver Springs, MD: National Council for the Social Studies.

National Council for the Social Studies. (1994). *Expectations of excellence: Curriculum standards for social studies*. Washington, DC: Author.

National Council of Teachers of English and International Reading Association. (1996). *Standards for the English language arts*. Urbana, IL: National Council of Teachers of English.

Sunal, C. S., & Haas, M. E. (2005). *Social studies for the elementary and middle grades: A constructivist approach* (2nd ed.). Boston: Allyn & Bacon.

Strategy 15

Establishing a Pluralist Approach to Content

DO A DEBATE

"Hi, Dad. You wanted to know what I learned in school today? Well, I learned that I am confused. We talked about the colonists and why they protested against England and taxes. But I wonder how the English felt about all of this?" queried Robert.

E ven the youngest of students often have very strong opinions on what they feel about certain issues. Kindergarteners can and do express how they are affected by and what their feelings are toward concerns, particularly those that directly affect them. For example, if the youngest are asked to give up snack or recess time, they have definite opinions about why they should have snack and recess. Teaching students to look at both sides of an issue and not just their own opinion or special interest is a challenge. This challenge can be met by providing students with strategies and activities that help them to think about alternative sides of an issue.

Sunal and Haas (2005) state that students can and should be taught ways and procedures that will help them identify and cope with issues and concerns. First, children should learn to identify the facts and then the issues and concerns. These issues and concerns should be in the format of questions. This way, students can understand that the answers are not absolutes but rather help learners to understand that issues contain multiple, sometimes conflicting viewpoints. Also, issues can be resolved through a variety of alternatives, but each and every alternative has consequences. Critical thinking, investigation, and deliberation follow, and obstacles. alternatives, and consequences are evaluated. Disagreement and debate may also follow because not everyone agrees on the alternative and consequences. Parker (2009) also reminds teachers that some controversies are factual—depending on the facts of a situation. Others are definitional—depending on the question. Teaching students to investigate and form opinions so that they are prepared and able to defend their ideas and beliefs is essential to establishing a pluralist approach to content. The process of this discussion and debate is what supports students in the development of critical-thinking skills (Wolk, 2003).

Please visit www.sagepub.com/lmelberstudy for the updated National Council of the Social Studies standards.

Curriculum Standards for Social Studies

- Strand IV: Individual Development & Identity
- Strand V: Individuals, Groups, & Institutions
- Strand X: Civic Ideals & Practices

Standards for the English Language Arts

Debates provide the opportunity for students to explore methods of effective communication. From vocabulary choice and speech content to clarity of speech and cadence, debate activities can tap into all areas of the language arts curriculum.

- Standard 4: Students adjust their use of spoken, written, and visual language (e.g., conventions, style, vocabulary) to communicate effectively with a variety of audiences and for different purposes.

- Standard 5: Students employ a wide range of strategies as they write and use different writing process elements appropriately to communicate with different audiences for a variety of purposes.

- Standard 7: Students conduct research on issues and interests by generating ideas and questions, and by posing problems. They gather, evaluate, and synthesize data from a variety of sources (e.g., print and nonprint texts, artifacts, people) to communicate their discoveries in ways that suit their purpose and audience.

- Standard 8: Students use a variety of technological and informational resources (e.g., libraries, databases, computer networks, video) to gather and synthesize information and to create and communicate knowledge.

- Standard 11: Students participate as knowledgeable, reflective, creative, and critical members of a variety of literacy communities.

- Standard 12: Students use spoken, written, and visual language to accomplish their own purposes (e.g., for learning, enjoyment, persuasion, and the exchange of information).

Technology Connection

Students may want to explore using a digital video camera to capture their debate. The video can be inexpensively burned onto individual DVDs for families to enjoy at home. (Be sure to procure parental permission before videotaping minors.)

Sources: National Council for the Social Studies, 1994; National Council of Teachers of English and International Reading Association, 1996.

KEY THEMES

Asking questions

Identifying components of an issue

Assessing the credibility of information

Determining the feasibility of alternatives

Evaluating the consequences of various alternatives

Taking a stand on a controversial issue

MATERIALS

Data sheet

PROCEDURES

Teachers can introduce the idea of varying opinions on a topic by an introductory discussion that asks students to state their opinion about an issue that is close to them, such as something in their school. Students can first be asked how they feel about the issue and then instructed to write their feelings and opinions as a personal journal entry. At this point, students should not be asked to share their opinions, but rather, teachers should instruct them in ways to consider research facts relating to their opinions. After students have researched facts, they should examine their original journal entry and see if they still hold the same belief about the issue. Next, they should be instructed in how to examine alternative viewpoints by continuing to research the issue. Such research could involve once again consulting print and nonprint resources. Also, students should be encouraged to speak with each other about what they believe. An interesting and different way that teachers can facilitate this is to have learners group themselves according to whether they agree or disagree with an issue or statement about the issue. Students pretend they are in a line. Those who agree with the issue stand at one end; those who disagree stand at the other end. Students who are unsure of their position on the issue stand in the middle. A rudimentary form of debate can begin. Students from each end of the line try to convince those in the middle to literally and figuratively join their side.

Learners can be challenged to record their original viewpoints, research, and resulting findings on a data sheet (see Figure 15.1 on p. 109). They can be asked to compare these sheets and continue to group and regroup themselves based on these comparisons. Teachers can then choose to have their classes divide themselves into debate teams that express opposing views.

Special Considerations

It is important to take care in the selection of topics for debate so that students are not presented with sensitive topics too complex to be treated appropriately during limited class time. Topics with religious or moral undertones may not be good choices for this type of activity. In addition, be sensitive to the fact that emotions from a class debate may spill over into students' social interactions, and thus, pick topics accordingly to avoid unnecessary discord.

Grade-Level Modifications

K–2nd Grade

Young learners can be encouraged to talk about their feelings and why they feel as they do. Teachers help by providing a supportive environment in which all are encouraged to participate. In addition, an entire class can be asked how they feel about an issue. This works well when they are asked to relate to and talk about things that are relevant to them personally. For example, students can be asked about such topics as whether they should have any responsibilities with regard to a family pet or whether they should have any responsibilities in their classroom. Teachers can help these young learners see both sides of these and other personal issues. Class discussion is essential.

3rd Grade–5th Grade

Completing a data sheet in which students are not only asked their opinions but to research facts about an issue or controversy is a way to assist this age group in grounding their opinions in facts and not just emotions. Expanding the data sheet information into written essays can also help learners clarify their opinions. Such essays should include a thesis or main opinion statement, reasons for the opinion, disproving of reasons that do not support the statement, and a conclusion. Finally, students can be challenged to form teams of those who have the same opinions to talk with teams that have different viewpoints. The reasons for the opinion recorded in the essays can serve as affirmative arguments, and the disproving statements can be used against the other team.

6th Grade–8th Grade

Students of this age group can be involved in a more formal oral presentation of their opinions. They should be encouraged to record their opinions and list pros and cons after they have done research as directed on the data sheet. Research should not be limited to print sources. They should be encouraged to talk with people who are involved with the issue, such as an environmentalist or scientist to discuss global warming. They should also be encouraged to read periodicals that have differing views. Many teachers are already aware of the value controversial topics bring to social studies instruction (Byford, Lennon, & Russell, 2009). Furthermore, Parker (2009) suggests that enduring public issues, such as poverty, human environment interaction, justice, peace, and diversity and unity can lead to the creation of issue-centered units and activities.

Meeting the Needs of English Learners

Since English learners sometimes have a limited understanding of literal words, it is important that they be assisted in comprehending the concepts involved in the issues being discussed and debated. Teachers and aides can serve as scribes to help these students comprehend and complete the requirements of the data sheet.

Meeting the Needs of Students With Special Needs

Students who have difficulty reading can be provided additional questions to guide their comprehension of resource texts. Also, they can be given additional time to complete the data sheet or be required to complete fewer sections. Assistive technology, such as text and screen reading software with adapted input, can be used to provide alternatives or supplements to printed information.

ASSESSMENT SUGGESTION

At the conclusion of this activity, students will be able to:

- Form an opinion based on factual evidence
- Defend this opinion
- Answer questions about the consequences of the actions resulting from this opinion

Students' entries on the data chart can be assessed using the following rubric:

Score	Criteria
4	Opinion is stated clearly, resources are effectively consulted and summarized, and defense for final opinion valid and validated.
3	Opinion is stated clearly, there are some concerns either with resources consulted or ideas summarized, and final opinion is somewhat validated and valid.
2	Opinion is stated somewhat clearly, there are major concerns with either resources consulted or ideas summarized, and final opinion is somewhat validated and valid.
1	Opinion stated is unclear, major concerns with resources and ideas summarized, and final opinion is unclear or invalid.

Children's Literature Connection

I Want an Iguana

By Karen Orloff

ISBN: 978–0399237178

This book for the youngest elementary students is told in note form. Alex tries to convince his mother that he needs to have a pet iguana. Opinions, values, evidence, and consequences are considered.

The Lincoln–Douglas Debates

By Brendan January

ISBN: 978–0516263359

This short text places the art of debating in historical context by describing seven debates between Lincoln and Douglas.

Talk the Talk: Speech and Debate Made Easy

By Alim Merali

ISBN: 978–0973868203

This book for older elementary school students is a practical guide on how to construct an argument and win a debate.

Quick Fact

While the format of today's presidential debates is different from the debates between that of Lincoln and Douglas in the 1800s, these modern debates trace their origin to the debates between these two individuals.

FIGURE 15.1   Do a Debate Sample Data Sheet   3rd–5th, 6th–8th

Name: _____

Topic: _____

My opinion:

_____

_____

_____

_____

_____

Research I did about this topic:

Source: _____

What I discovered:

_____

_____

_____

_____

Source: _____

What I discovered:

_____

_____

_____

_____

(Continued)

FIGURE 15.1 (Continued)	3rd–5th, 6th–8th

Source: _____

What I discovered:

_____

_____

_____

_____

What my sources said that was the same:

_____

_____

_____

_____

What my sources said that was different:

_____

_____

_____

_____

Has my opinion changed? Why or why not?

_____

_____

_____

_____

_____

REFERENCES

Byford, J., Lennon, S., & Russell, W. B. (2009). Teaching controversial issues in the social studies: A research study of high school teachers. *The Clearing House, 82*(4), 165–171.

National Council for the Social Studies. (1994). *Expectations of excellence: Curriculum standards for social studies*. Washington, DC: Author.

National Council of Teachers of English and International Reading Association. (1996). *Standards for the English language arts*. Urbana, IL: National Council of Teachers of English.

Parker, W. C. (2009). *Social studies in elementary education*. Upper Saddle River, NJ: Prentice Hall.

Sunal, C. S., & Haas, M. E. (2005). *Social studies for the elementary and middle grades: A constructivist approach* (2nd ed.). Boston: Allyn & Bacon.

Wolk, S. (2003). Teaching for critical literacy in social studies. *The Social Studies, 94*(3), 101–106.

UNIT IV
Past and Present

National social studies curriculum standards (National Council for the Social Studies, 1994) emphasize the importance of developing historical perspective. However, many students are currently receiving social studies instruction that focuses simply on basic historical facts such as isolated names and dates without the rich context that surrounds these names, dates, and events (Vogler & Virtue, 2007).

Working with primary sources can provide an authentic view into the past that informational text does not (Morris, 2002). Letters may express genuine emotion and beliefs more accurately than a chapter in a textbook. A photo of a clothing iron made of cast iron does not accurate belie the difficulty of its use the same way handling such an object would. For students, these experiences with the genuine artifact will be a great help. In this unit, instructional techniques are highlighted that will support students in evaluating primary sources and gleaning critical information from them to better understand lifeways of the past. Through examination of primary sources—defining purpose, identifying bias, and determining source—students model historical thinking and analysis in line with practicing historians (De La Paz & MacArthur, 2003).

Connecting with the world outside of the classroom, both through these primary sources and through quality connections with the community itself, can support students in discovering the relevance of historic events and lifeways to their own (Morris, 2006). This personal connection can in turn support cognitive gains and help students add context to the names and dates of traditional history curriculum.

REFERENCES

De La Paz, S., & MacArthur, C. (2003). Knowing the how and why of history: Expectations for secondary students with and without learning disabilities. *Learning Disability Quarterly, 26*,142–154.

Morris, R. V. (2002). Use primary sources to develop a soap opera: As the Civil War turns. *The Social Studies, 93*(2), 53–56.

Morris, R. V. (2006). The land of hope: Third-grade students use a walking tour to explore their community. *The Social Studies, 97*(3), 129–132.

National Council for the Social Studies. (1994). *Expectations of excellence: Curriculum standards for social studies*. Washington, DC: Author.

Vogler, K. E., & Virtue, D. (2007). "Just the facts, ma'am": Teaching social studies in the era of standards and high-stakes testing. *The Social Studies, 98*(2), 54–58.

Strategy 16

Incorporating Historical Reenactment

MAKING BUTTER

"My arm is tired!" complained Kia.

"Give it to me then," said Stacy as she grabbed for the jar. "I haven't had a turn yet."

Kia begrudgingly passed the small jar over to Stacy and dramatically rubbed her arm. As Stacy shook with vigor, the other students waited patiently for their turn. They heard shouts of excitement from the other groups and were impatient to see the same change occur with their cream that they saw happening in the other groups.

"Okay, I'm tired now too!" Stacy said. "I want to see if it's done yet!" The group crowded around Stacy as she carefully opened the jar.

"It's a lump! It's a lump!" shouted Jason.

Kia frowned a bit at the small lump of butter floating in the jar. "That's it?" she whispered to Stacy. "That's sure a lot of work for just a little bit of butter."

O ne way that historians learn about the past is through careful reconstructions. They might learn how to construct an ancient boat by replicating the process with the same type of materials and tools. They may re-create recipes or baking methods. Incorporating re-creations or reenactments into the classroom not only allows students to be actively involved in learning, but also provides opportunities to gain information that goes beyond straight content. Museums have long used historical reenactments as an opportunity to actively engage learners in social science content (Van Scotter, White, Hartoonian, & Davis, 2007). This might include the fatigue of doing manual labor, the extended amount of time to complete something without modern conveniences, or the reality of fewer choices than in the modern day. Few if any students are familiar with a self-sustaining lifestyle. Even students who are part of an agricultural family are more likely to live on farms that specialize in one or two crops, complete with a number of modern conveniences that facilitate the business.

The butter-making activity is especially successful with students. For students to really understand important historical events, it is also important to understand the day-to-day life of people who lived through this time. Doing so through physical reenactment can result in tremendous learning gains (Putnam & Rommel-Esham, 2004). Some children, especially those from urban areas, may be unaware that butter will form from agitated cream. Even students who know about the origin of butter theoretically can learn first-hand the physical work that creating butter entails. Most important, making butter is relevant to even the youngest child. Butter is something most children have daily access to, and this activity allows them to tap into a parallel lifestyle element of the past.

Sources: National Council for the Social Studies, 1994; National Council of Teachers of English and International Reading Association, 1996.

Please visit www.sagepub.com/lmelberstudy for the updated National Council of the Social Studies standards.

Curriculum Standards for Social Studies

- Strand II: Time, Continuity, & Change
- Strand III: People, Places, & Environments

Standards for the English Language Arts

Students will develop expository writing skills through the completion of the data sheet. Sharing their discoveries with their peers supports oral language skills.

- Standard 5:   Students employ a wide range of strategies as they write and use different writing process elements appropriately to communicate with different audiences for a variety of purposes.

Technology Connection

The activity is likely to prompt many questions about the formation of butter that the average person may find difficult to answer! The site http://www.webexhibits.org/butter/index.html has an exceptional amount of information on how butter is formed, the history of butter, and the role of butter in global cultures.

KEY THEMES

Re-creating activities of past

Making observations

Comparing and contrasting the past with the present

MATERIALS

Small, clear plastic jars with lids (one per group of three to four students)

Heavy whipping cream (approximately eight ounces per four groups, depending on jar size)

Data sheets

Pencil/paper

PROCEDURES

When heavy whipping cream is agitated in a jar by shaking, butter will form. By taking part in this activity, students learn just how hard everyday activities and chores of the past could be.

The procedure for this activity will depend on the grade level as well as students' past experiences. If it is not likely that they will know butter will form from agitated cream, it is best to use the prediction and result model described in the following for younger grades. If students are likely to know the result either due to conducting the activity in years past or because of a familiarity with agriculture and the dairy industry, it is better to have them take part in the activity with a focus on making the process more efficient or comparing different approaches to the process. This will parallel the reality of how, over time, we as a society have improved technology to lighten our workload.

Adding marbles can increase the agitation and cause the butter to form more rapidly. Leaving more air in the jar will also result in greater agitation with each shake. Students may also want to compare the use of regular whipping cream with heavy whipping cream. The addition of salt can be another experiment.

However the activity is conducted, it is important to finish the activity with a discussion of how making butter using this method is different from how the majority of students access butter today. Many students find it tiring to shake the jar, and others are surprised that such a small amount is created from such hard work. As students gain understanding of how lifeways of the past are different from their own, they can better grasp the context surrounding important historical events.

GRADE-LEVEL MODIFICATIONS

K–2nd Grade

This age group is the least likely to know that butter will form from cream. Capitalize on this by using the provided data sheet (see Figure 16.1 on p. 116), which asks students to predict what will happen, record their observations, and share their opinions about the taste of the product. For students who are not able to write on their own, they can dictate answers to a teacher or parent volunteer.

3rd Grade–5th Grade

Depending on where students live, this age group may or may not know that butter will form from cream. For those students who know butter will form, encourage comparison between the butter and margarine of today with that formed through the activity. After making the butter in class, create a data sheet that asks students to compare the taste of two to three modern-day equivalents. Many students may be used to salted butter and find the butter they created is blander than what they are familiar with at home.

6th Grade–8th Grade

Healthy competition at this grade level can really spark an interest in learning. Provide students with a variety materials to design the most efficient shaking process.

Materials include jars of different sizes and items to agitate the cream, such as clean marbles. Keeping the assigned amount of cream standard, encourage students to come up with the method that will result in butter formation with the least amount of time spent shaking. Further discussion can tie to the invention of the butter churn as well as modern processing methods.

Meeting the Needs of English Learners

The re-creation itself will support English learners by creating a context-rich environment. The partner format of the experience will also be supportive of English learners. In addition, the focus on group collaboration and kinesthetic activity is a good match for the needs of English learners. Additional support can be provided to English learners by creating a word bank containing vocabulary students need to support completion of the data sheet. Allowing images rather than simply narrative text can be another helpful modification.

Meeting the Needs of Students With Special Needs

Students with attention deficits or who otherwise need a great deal of kinesthetic activity often excel at this activity. Their energy level is rewarded by more rapid formation of butter! Allowing the option to complete the data sheet as a group can support students with learning disabilities who may find the narrative portion tedious. For students with motor difficulties, shaking the jar without dropping it may prove difficult. Double-stick tape can facilitate holding the object, and selecting plastic jars that can drop without breaking will be imperative.

Assessment Suggestion

At the conclusion of the activity, students will be able to:

- Make butter from cream using simple agitation
- Observe as cream changes into butter
- Compare and contrast how past methods of making butter are different from how students procure butter

Students' data sheets can be assessed using a simple rubric such as the following:

Score	Criteria
4	All sections of the data sheet are complete with exceptional detail and insight.
3	All sections are complete with an acceptable level of detail.
2	Most of the sections are complete with an acceptable amount of detail, or all sections completed with significant errors.
1	Few of the sections are complete, or multiple errors present.

Children's Literature Connection

The Butter Man
    By Elizabeth Alalou
    ISBN: 1580891276
    This book provides insight into the Moroccan culture as well as taps into themes of fighting world hunger.

Quick Fact

Scholars believe that butter has been around for 4,000 years. The very earliest types of butter churns were bags made from goat skins. Shaking the bags agitated the cream to form butter. Later, settlers who traveled the Oregon Trail learned by accident that by tying barrels of cream to the wagon, the natural bumps and bangs of the trail would do the butter churning for them.

FIGURE 16.1   "What Will Happen?" Sample Data Sheet   K–2nd

Draw a picture of your jar before you begin shaking:

Draw a picture of your jar after you were done shaking:

Describe what happened to the cream:

_____

_____

_____

How does it taste?

_____

Would you want to do this every day?   _____ Yes   _____ No

Why or why not?

_____

_____

_____

REFERENCES

National Council for the Social Studies. (1994). *Expectations of excellence: Curriculum standards for social studies*. Washington, DC: Author.

National Council of Teachers of English and International Reading Association. (1996). *Standards for the English language arts*. Urbana, IL: National Council of Teachers of English.

Putnam, E., & Rommel-Esham, K. (2004). Using oral history to study change: An integrated approach. *The Social Studies, 95*(5), 201–205.

Van Scotter, R., White, W. E., Hartoonian, H. M., Davis, J. E. (2007). A gateway to social studies through topical history. *Social Studies, 98*(6), 231–235.

Strategy 17

Personal Correspondence as a Primary Source

POSTCARD EXPLORATION

The students sorted through the postcards they had been given. They knew to touch gently and had all washed their hands before beginning the activity.

"Here's another postcard addressed to 'Elva,' but she has a different last name."

"That's weird," Jose said with a furrowed brow. "They both have the same address, so it must be the same person."

"Maybe she got married," offered Julie helpfully. The teacher smiled to herself. Her great-grandmother Elva had actually been married three times!

Julie and Jose smiled, and all three of the team members began to write enthusiastically on their data sheets.

"This is so funny," comment Jin. "They're writing about our city, San Francisco!"

"It's dated 1913! Wow, that was before my grandma was alive," commented Jose as he squinted to read the tiny handwriting. "Listen to this! She wrote: 'The houses are so unusual, all very close together and skinny. We had a dandy time at the dance, wish you had come.'"

"That's funny," said Jin. "I never thought about our town that way, but I guess she is right."

"Yeah, it's funny that dancing was popular then just like it is now," responded Julie.

"I'm sure they danced a lot differently," laughed Jose. "And I wouldn't be caught dead using the word *dandy!*"

Written correspondence such as letters and postcards can support students in learning about the past in a personally relevant manner. These primary sources provide students with insight into the past and the opportunity to develop empathy and greater understanding of a historical event through first-person narrative (McCormick, 2004), as well as aid in the development of historical perspective (Nash, Crabtree, & National History Task Force, 1996).

When primary sources are difficult to understand or are a poor match for a child's developmental level, it is unlikely that a quality learning experience will occur. It is also important to incorporate items that students will be able to connect with personally and find interesting (Chapin, 2006). Using postcards or letters is way to bring primary source data into the classroom in a way that is relevant and understandable to students. They also will allow students to explore the role of bias in primary sources and how to use that bias as information rather than disregard the source altogether.

Sources: National Council for the Social Studies, 1994; National Council of Teachers of English and International Reading Association, 1996.

Please visit www.sagepub.com/lmelberstudy for the updated National Council of the Social Studies standards.

Curriculum Standards for Social Studies

- Strand I: Culture
- Strand II: Time, Continuity, & Change
- Strand IV: Individual Development & Identify

Standards for the English Language Arts

Oral interviews support students in comprehension of the spoken word as well as effective methods of orally communicating themselves. Allowing students to use their first language during the project is further supportive of language arts development.

- Standard 4:   Students adjust their use of spoken, written, and visual language (e.g., conventions, style, vocabulary) to communicate effectively with a variety of audiences and for different purposes.

- Standard 5:   Students employ a wide range of strategies as they write and use different writing process elements appropriately to communicate with different audiences for a variety of purposes.

Technology Connection

Students can learn more about vintage postcards as well as see images from their home state at the following Web site: http://www.rootsweb.ancestry.com/~usgenweb/special/ppcs/ppcs.html.

KEY THEMES

Making observations

Analyzing postcards

Making inferences based on data

Communicating explanations and interpretations

MATERIALS

All that is required for this activity is a collection of written postcards. You may already have your own collection. Another option is to ask friends and family to mail you child-friendly postcards whenever they are on a trip to build a collection. A third option is to purchase historic postcards at a swap meet or flea market. Traditionally, postcards with writing, postmarks, creases and stains lose collectable value and are available in bulk at very low cost. Whatever the source, it will be important to determine that the messages and images are appropriate for young eyes. You might also choose to use the four sample postcards provided until you can achieve a larger collection of your own (see Figure 17.1 on p. 123).

PROCEDURES

Explain to students that one way social scientists learn about the past is by studying artifacts and other primary sources from long ago. Just as they read letters and postcards to learn about their friends and families, reading postcards from long ago can provide us with information on lifeways of the past.

Before asking students to work independently, it is best to project an image of a postcard in front of the class and lead a preparatory discussion. Younger students will likely benefit from a lengthy discussion. Older students may need just a little orientation, leaving much discussion for them to do in their groups. The presentation can be done with whatever technology is present in the classroom. Copying a postcard onto a transparency and using with an overhead projector is one option. Scanning the image and using an LCD projector is a more technologically advanced option. You will want to use both the image and the message side of the postcard. Lead a class discussion about the postcard image first. Potential questions include:

- What can we tell from the picture about when this card was sent?
- Does the image show a city or natural location?
- What in the image do students find most interesting?
- Do students see anything in the image that reminds them of their own city?
- Is there anything in the image very different from students' own experiences?

Next, lead a discussion regarding the message of the postcard. If using vintage cards, personal handwriting and faded ink may be hard to read. In this case, transcribe the message using a basic font so students can observe the original handwriting for context, but can use the transcription to read for understanding. Potential questions include:

- What is the message about?
- How are the sender and the recipient related?
- When was the postcard sent?
- How is the message similar to one that a student might receive on a postcard today?
- How is the address different from your own address?
- Is there a postmark? What information does this provide?

After leading a class discussion, modeling the analytical process, place students in groups of four. You will provide each student with his or her own postcard, but encourage students to share and discuss their postcard with the group before completing their data sheet. After setting aside 10 minutes for open discussion, instruct students to begin work on their data sheet (see Figure 17.2 on p. 127), recording the discoveries that came from their analysis. After they have completed their data sheet, provide students with the template (see Figure 17.3 on p. 129) to create an original postcard.

With their assigned postcard in front of them as reference, instruct students to write a response to the sender as if they were the addressee, staying true to the details they gleaned through their analysis. To provide students with plenty of time to do their best work, without fatigue, it might be helpful for third to fifth graders to do this second part of the activity on a subsequent day.

GRADE-LEVEL MODIFICATIONS

K–2nd Grade

Because students in this grade range are likely to be emergent readers, the handwriting of personal letters may be difficult for them to decipher. Options are to conduct the activity with a few adult helpers who can read the cards to the students and lead a group discussion rather than having to work independently and record their responses on a data sheet. Another option is to ask friends to send postcards from other states using simple language and easy-to-read handwriting that will be readable by emerging readers. Conducting the first part as a class discussion and instead focusing on the response card as the individually conducted activity can be a helpful modification.

3rd Grade–5th Grade and 6th Grade–8th Grade

Students in both of these grade ranges will be able to read the letter or postcard messages and decipher what the message can tell us about what was happening at the time, and a little about the history of the individual. Transcriptions may be necessary on the most faded or flowery handwriting styles. For sixth- to eighth-grade students, holding only a brief prediscussion is recommended to encourage them to develop their own questions for analysis. Listing a few sample questions from those listed previously on a board or a handout can serve as a starting place.

MEETING THE NEEDS OF ENGLISH LEARNERS

Many English learners are more fluent in conversational vocabulary than academic language. Reviewing letters or postcards, students are likely to encounter vocabulary they are already familiar with. By working in groups, students can also support each other with reading comprehension. The short length of the documents is a manageable task that is less likely to discourage English learners than an entire textbook chapter. If you are fortunate to have students with friends and family living and traveling outside of the country, including foreign postcards as part of the lesson can be an exciting extension.

MEETING THE NEEDS OF STUDENTS WITH SPECIAL NEEDS

Students with learning disabilities may have even more difficulty than their peers in reading the personal handwriting on a postcard. Creating a typed version of the message using easy-to-read font will aid in the reading portion without taking away from the analysis aspect of the activity. Students with disabilities in the area of fine motor skills may benefit from placing the postcards inside an 8½ by 11–inch plastic sleeve, which may be easier to turn over than the smaller postcards.

ASSESSMENT SUGGESTION

At the conclusion of the activity, students will be able to:

- Make careful observations of postcards
- Analyze messages and images from postcards
- Make inferences about senders and recipients of postcards
- Communicate interpretations through postcard creations

Students' final data sheets can be assessed using the following rubric:

Score	Criteria
4	All sections of the data sheet are complete with exceptional detail and insight.
3	All sections are complete with an acceptable level of detail.
2	Most of the sections are complete with an acceptable amount of detail, or all sections completed with significant errors.
1	Few of the sections are complete, or multiple errors present.

Students' original postcards can be assessed using the following rubric:

Score	Image	Message/Address
4	Illustration is complete, with exceptional detail and appropriate for timeframe of original postcard.	Address is correct format. Message is in line with time period and content of original postcard, and contains extensive detail.
3	Illustration is complete but lacks either detail or color.	Address is in correct format. Message is in line with time period and content of original card but with limited detail.
2	Illustration is complete but lacks both detail and color.	Address and message are both present, but errors with format, time period, or content are present.
1	Incomplete illustration.	Only one of the two elements are present, or there are considerable errors with both sections.

Children's Literature Connection

The series "Postcards From" focuses on children sending postcards home from places all around the world describing their experiences. Titles include travels to China, Mexico, Australia, Japan, and others. Search available titles at: http://steckvaughn.harcourtachieve.com/en-US/steckvaughn.htm.

Quick Fact

From 1901 to 1907, the back of a postcard was reserved for only the address of the person it was being sent to. Senders were often relegated to writing any message over the picture on the front of the card. After 1907, divided backs allowed room for an address and a message. The term for the study and collections of postcards is *deltiology*.

FIGURE 17.1   Sample Postcards

To Miss Elva Caylor

Nov. 24, 1911

Houston, Texas

How is Elvie by now? We are having lots of fun. But the heat is fierce for us. I lost 7 lbs in 6 days time.

Mrs. Collier

(Continued)

FIGURE 17.1 (Continued)

Miss Elva Caylor

July 22, 1911

Dear Elva—This is where we are going Wednesday. It is one finest bath house on the Pacific Coast. Mornings are perfectly grand here—fog and cool until ten usually and sea breeze in afternoons. Have only had three or four hot days. How is the weather there? Loads of fruit and vegetables here. I'm sure I shall miss them when I come home and the pretty lawns and flowers and big trees. Would like to hear from you (address). Love, Blanche

To Mrs E. C. Bowen

Nov. 3, 1909

This leaves me in Banan with Mike. We had a fair trip down, but the steers were mean to lead. Hope you are well.

From Rea

(Continued)

FIGURE 17.1   (Continued)

1686   Mount of the Holy Cross, Colorado.

To Elva Bowen

Sept. 28, 1919

Do try and come to the dance. Bill and you will have a dandy time. L. T. S.

(upside down . . . Earl says do come!)

Source: Postcards courtesy of the Davis Family.

FIGURE 17.2   Postcard Stories Sample Data Sheet 1   3rd–5th, 6th–8th

Historian: _____

Briefly describe the image:

_____

_____

_____

_____

What elements of the image are similar to today?

_____

_____

_____

_____

What elements of the image are different from today?

_____

_____

_____

Briefly describe the message:

_____

_____

_____

(Continued)

FIGURE 17.2   (Continued)   3rd–5th, 6th–8th

What elements of the message are similar to a postcard you might receive today?

_____

_____

_____

What elements of the message are different from a postcard you might receive today?

_____

_____

_____

Briefly describe the address:

_____

_____

_____

What elements are similar to the way mail is addressed today?

_____

_____

_____

What elements are different from the way mail is addressed today?

_____

_____

_____

FIGURE 17.3 Postcard Response Sample Data Sheet 2   K–2nd, 3rd–5th, 6th–8th

Historian: _____

Select one of the postcards. Pretend you are the addressee and write a response to the post-card you have selected. You will also want to create an image that you think would be relevant and accurate for the time as well as the location where your addressee lives.

Message

Image

REFERENCES

Chapin, J. R. (2006). *Elementary social studies: A practical guide* (6th ed.). Boston: Allyn & Bacon.

McCormick, T. M. (2004). Letters from Trenton, 1776: Teaching with primary sources. *Social Studies and the Young Learner, 17*(2), 5–12.

Nash, G., Crabtree, E., & National History Task Force. (1996). *National standards for history, basic edition.* Los Angeles: National Center for History in Schools.

National Council for the Social Studies. (1994). *Expectations of excellence: Curriculum standards for social studies.* Washington, DC: Author.

National Council of Teachers of English and International Reading Association. (1996). *Standards for the English language arts.* Urbana, IL: National Council of Teachers of English.

Systematic Artifact Investigation

Strategy 18

"This is *so* heavy!" Jeanne commented as she held the cast-iron key. At five inches long, it definitely wasn't something she could picture wearing around her neck. "I think we discovered the main drawback of this item!"

"Let's do the part about its modern match—obviously, it's the modern day key," Chris said as he started to write on his sheet.

Casey had been very quiet and thoughtful for the last few minutes, so when he spoke, everyone was interested in what he had to say. "We can put down more than just a smaller version of the key," he said.

"Like what?" Sophia asked.

"Well," said Casey, a little embarrassed that the group had all their attention focused on him. "My dad works at a museum, and he uses his ID badge as a key. He swipes it in this machine and the door opens."

"Yeah!" said Sophia. "My mom works at the hospital, and she has one too!"

"We don't use keys," said Jeanne sadly. "We just go into our house through the garage." Her disappointment at not having a "key story" was evident.

"That's another one! A garage door opener is like a key too!" shouted Chris.

Sophia beamed, and they all bent down to complete their data sheets. "I bet the owner of this key would be shocked to see how many different types of keys we have today," she laughed.

For researchers, careful analysis of artifacts can provide a detailed window into lifeways of the past. Using artifacts as a primary source ties to the authentic work of social scientists who may use the study of material culture in their own research. Specifically, students take part in study "through artifacts of the beliefs—values, ideas, attitudes, and assumptions—of a particular community or society at a given time" (Prown, 1982, p. 1). At the center of material culture is the artifact, or an object either created by humans or modified by humans (Prown, 1982).

In this chapter, students will be focusing on the information that can be obtained through careful study of material culture. Students will be observing two artifacts or replica artifacts with similar uses that come from different time periods. Using a graphic organizer (Gallavan & Kottler, 2007), students will identify how the items are similar as well as differences between the artifacts. Data indicate that students are interested in the past generally, but may be more interested in the recent past of their parents and grandparents (Whitting, 1998).

When taught using traditional methods, many students find that study of the past lacks relevance to their own lives, which can in turn compromise cognitive gains. This careful investigation of everyday items can lead from discussions of personal and family identity to broader discussions of cultural identity (Whitting, 1998).

Please visit www.sagepub.com/lmelberstudy for the updated National Council of the Social Studies standards.

Curriculum Standards for Social Studies

- Strand I: Culture
- Strand II: Time, Continuity, & Change
- Strand III: People, Places, & Environments

Standards for the English Language Arts

Throughout the data collection phase, students are relying on language arts to communicate with their peers. Completed data sheets synthesize student ideas and inferences.

- Standard 5:   Students employ a wide range of strategies as they write and use different writing process elements appropriately to communicate with different audiences for a variety of purposes.

Technology Connection

After completing their data sheets, students may want to explore the Internet for more information on their artifacts. Sites used will depend on the objects selected by the individual teacher, so an exhaustive list is beyond the scope of this work. By using the "search images" command on many Internet search engines, you can quickly identify the best search words to match the artifact of study.

Sources: National Council for the Social Studies, 1994; National Council of Teachers of English and International Reading Association, 1996.

KEY THEMES

Making observations
Comparing and contrasting past with the present
Communicating explanations and interpretations

Materials

Paired objects from past and present (one pair per group of three)

Data sheets

Pens/pencils

Demonstration object

Procedures

Start the activity by explaining to students that many social science researchers focus on objects as the center of their research. By carefully exploring, investigation, and observing objects, they learn about an earlier society or way of life. For example, what an object is made from can provide information on how a society relied on different natural resources. The structure or wear of an item can provide clues as to how the item was used.

Acquiring Items

The most cost-efficient way to acquire objects for this activity is by a visit to an elderly relative's house or a nearby garage sale. A visit to my own grandmother's house resulted in the loan of an American flag with only 48 stars, a cast-iron pressing iron from the 1800s being used as a doorstop, and a cast-iron curling iron that was heated by direct contact with fire. A garage sale can yield a stack of 8-track cassettes, a cell phone the size of a brick, or platform shoes from the 1970s. Swap meets and online auctions are additional sources for the real thing at a nominal cost. If the goal is to tie to a particular time period, inexpensive replicas can often be purchased from museums or other educational organizations. Two helpful sites to browse are:

Panther Primitives
Products range from full-sized Civil War era tents to arrowhead replicas, children's toys, and cooking utensils in line with those used along the Oregon Trail. Visit www.pantherprimitives.com.

Colonial Williamsburg
This living history site has a number of products available through its online gift shop. Replicas of Colonial Era games, writing utensils, and even publications can be purchased at reasonable prices. Visit www.history.org.

Prepare students for carefully observing an object by modeling a sample analysis. Select something from the classroom that students are familiar with. Perhaps it is a well-worn teacher's edition of a textbook or a dusty slide projector unused for the last two decades. Ask students to make inferences about how the item might have been used or who might have used it based on their observations.

After the group discussion, place students in groups of three. For each group, provide students with an object from the past (or replica) and a modern equivalent. Sample pairings with items likely to be in your home might be:

- Rotary phone and cell phone
- Metal key and card key
- Glass/sand egg timer and digital timer
- Flag with 48 stars and flag with 50 stars

Provide students with time to investigate the objects as a group, and circulate between groups to facilitate discussion as appropriate. After a period of group discussion, students should complete their data sheet (see Figure 18.1) on their own. Although they may likely agree with their group members, completing the data sheet as an individual allows for different interpretations and opinions. After students have had time to complete their data sheets, provide each group with an opportunity to share their objects with the class and report out their findings. Time should be allotted for all students in the group to share, inclusive of dissenting views.

GRADE-LEVEL MODIFICATIONS

K–2nd Grade

Students at this grade level will benefit from objects that hold personal relevance. Toys, household items, and cooking utensils are examples of items that students will already have experiences with. In addition, restructuring the sample data sheet to focus on only a few differences and similarities and a word bank will help with developing language skills.

3rd Grade–5th Grade and 6th Grade–8th Grade

For these students, an interesting modification is to only provide them with the historic item and leave identification of the modern item up to them. This open-ended approach to completing the data sheet will encourage students to tap into their own experiences as well as result in a greater range of responses, much like the vignette illustrates.

MEETING THE NEEDS OF ENGLISH LEARNERS

As discussed in previous chapters, the use of concrete objects will support English learners in vocabulary development as well as provide context that will be critical to full understanding. The addition of a word bank to the data sheet or as a separate page will support students in creating a thorough narrative on the data sheet. Selection of objects familiar to a variety of households and avoidance of items that may be unfamiliar to students from culturally diverse backgrounds will also be important.

MEETING THE NEEDS OF STUDENTS WITH SPECIAL NEEDS

The context of using authentic objects will support students with learning disabilities in creating meaning. To support students with limited fine motor skills, it will be important to select objects that can withstand accidental drops and not be too heavy for handling. The emphasis on exploration by touch will support students with low vision. Students who may have difficulty self-motivating often find the novelty of hands-on experience with authentic objects can support effort and motivation.

ASSESSMENT SUGGESTION

At the conclusion of the activity, students will be able to:

- Make observations of artifacts
- Compare and contrast the past with the present through artifact investigation
- Communicate explanations and interpretations based on analysis

Students' final data sheets can be assessed using the following rubric:

Score	Criteria
4	All sections of the data sheet are complete with exceptional detail and insight.
3	All sections are complete with an acceptable level of detail.
2	Most of the sections are complete with an acceptable amount of detail, or all sections are complete with significant errors.
1	Few of the sections are complete, or multiple errors are present.

Children's Literature Connection

It is best to select books most closely linked to the objects that are selected for study. A series that is helpful in providing general information on the daily activities and household items of the past is the "*If You Lived . . .*" series. Explore different titles at Scholastic's Web site, http://www2.scholastic.com/browse/index.jsp.

Quick Fact

There are different opinions on how old something must be to be considered an antique. A range of 50 to 100 years old is commonly used for most objects. Some experts classify automobiles, objects related to automobiles, or other heavily used items, as an antique at an age of 25 years or older.

FIGURE 18.1   Then and Now Sample Data Sheet   3rd–5th, 6th–8th

Historian: _____

Historic artifact: _____

Sketch:

(Continued)

FIGURE 18.1   (Continued)   3rd–5th, 6th–8th

Description:

_____

_____

_____

_____

Modern equivalent: _____

	Benefits	Drawbacks/Challenges
Historic Version		
Modern Equivalent		

Area of further research:

_____

_____

REFERENCES

Gallavan, N. P., & Kottler, E. (2007). Eight types of graphic organizers for empowering social studies students and teachers. *The Social Studies, 98*(7), 117–123.

National Council for the Social Studies. (1994). *Expectations of excellence: Curriculum standards for social studies.* Washington, DC: Author.

National Council of Teachers of English and International Reading Association. (1996). *Standards for the English language arts.* Urbana, IL: National Council of Teachers of English.

Prown, J. D. (1982). Mind in matter: An introduction to material culture theory and method author(s). *Winterthur Portfolio, 17*(1), 1–19.

Whitting, N. C. (1998). Archaeology and intercultural education in the elementary grades: An example from Minnesota. *The Social Studies, 89*(6), 254–259.

Relevant Approaches to Economics

Strategy 19

The students sat at a table with five different product advertisements in front of them. The ads were all from the 1950s and were focused on various household items such as vacuum cleaners, cake mix, and cleaning supplies.

"Why is she so dressed up to clean the house?" Jaycee asked. "She's wearing a dress and high heels!"

"That's how they dressed all the time back then. That's what my mom said," answered Josh with a frown. "I think it's pretty silly. I'm sure she'll trip over the vacuum."

"She sure looks happy though. I bet having a vacuum means her work goes faster," commented Deshaun.

"More time to do her makeup!" laughed Jaycee.

"They all seem to talk about time," comment Josh. "Look, this one says that the cleaning scrub will cut cleaning time in half. The other one says the cake mix will help you bake a cake in half the time."

"So I guess the most important thing to selling products in the 1950s was pointing out how much time you could save," summarized Josh.

"And still look fabulous while doing it!" laughed Jaycee.

Economics may not be a topic that many of us remember fondly. That's likely because our first experiences with economic concepts in school lacked context and personally relevant connections. Most agree that the earlier students learn economic concepts, the better prepared they are for important financial decisions as adults. With a clear rationale for the importance of economic studies, all that's left is the creation of experiences that build enthusiasm along with understanding.

Economic studies are a critical part of a complete social studies curriculum (National Council for the Social Studies, 1994). Personally relevant connections to students' lives will make economic concepts understandable to even the youngest learner. Deciding to save or spend one's allowance, being inspired by an advertisement to ask for a toy, sharing limited candy (Marks & Davis, 2006), or helping out with a family-owned business are just a few examples of how economic principles may affect everyday life.

The role of advertising in modern society is a dominant one. There is extensive literature confirming that carefully crafted advertisements affect consumers and inspire them to action. This activity asks students to think critically about advertising techniques through ad analysis and creation. This analysis opportunity can build understanding of how advertising messages can influence purchasing behavior.

Please visit
www.sagepub.com/lmelberstudy
for the updated National Council of
the Social Studies standards.

Curriculum Standards for Social Studies

- Strand II: Time, Continuity, & Change
- Strand X: Global Connections

Standards for the English Language Arts

This activity provides particular emphasis on vocabulary development as well as the importance of clarity in all communication.

- Standard 1: Students read a wide range of print and nonprint texts to build an understanding of texts, of themselves, and of the cultures of the United States and the world; to acquire new information; to respond to the needs and demands of society and the workplace; and for personal fulfillment. Among these texts are fiction and nonfiction, classic and contemporary works.

- Standard 5: Students employ a wide range of strategies as they write and use different writing process elements appropriately to communicate with different audiences for a variety of purposes.

Technology Connection

There are a nearly infinite number of Web sites featuring vintage advertisements. These can support class discussion as well as serve as the resource for ads you would like to use for this activity.

Sources: National Council for the Social Studies, 1994; National Council of Teachers of English and International Reading Association, 1996.

KEY THEMES

Analyzing advertisements

Comparing and contrasting the past with the present

Exploring economic themes

MATERIALS

Pens/pencils

Modern example of an advertisement

Reproductions of vintage product advertisements

Colored pencils/markers

Large, white construction paper (9 × 12 inches)

PROCEDURES

Begin the activity by displaying a modern print advertisement in front of the class. Lead a class discussion on how the advertisement would encourage someone to purchase the item. Support students in identifying the facts of the advertisements as well as the persuasive elements. Encourage them to identify elements of the advertisement that are well matched to the current era as well as contemporary issues and themes. For example, a product that boasts environmentally sound packaging is well-tied to the current societal emphasis on reducing waste and recycling.

After students have practiced these analytical processes as a whole class, place them in groups of two to four depending on the number of vintage advertisements that are available. Assigning each group a different advertisement is one way to do it, although the activity is equally effective if the same advertisement is used with each group. Using the whole-class preparation discussion as a model, have students analyze and discuss the vintage advertisements. A helpful element to incorporate is a small 3 by 5 inch card that lists the year of the advertisement and several important elements of the time period. For example, in the 1950s, many homemakers were looking for products to help them bake, clean, and otherwise take care of their homes more efficiently. How does an advertisement for a cake mix connect with that key theme? In the 1960s, more women were entering the workforce and taking on responsibilities more in line with those that were traditionally male. How might an advertisement from this time highlight the item for sale in a way that reflects critical issues of this time period?

For a final project, have students create an original advertisement. You can either allow students to select a product themselves or, if this proves too overwhelming, assign products. Ask students to create an original advertisement on a large piece of construction paper. A complete advertisement should include:

- An image of the product
- A product description
- Benefits
- Pricing information

The product should also be placed in a context in line with key societal themes as developmentally appropriate.

A great extension of the activity is to incorporate advertisements from other countries during the whole-class or small-group instruction. Even if students are not able to translate the text of the ad, the picture of the product and supporting images can be compared to historic and modern ads from the United States for a similar or related product.

GRADE-LEVEL MODIFICATIONS

K–2nd Grade

This activity is best done as a whole-group discussion. Share one or two advertisements with students, and discuss as a class what are the key parts of the advertisement that would make students want to buy the item. Advertisements for toys, sodas, or sweets might be the most relevant choices for students of this age. As a class, assign students a modern-day object and instruct them to use their drawing skills to create a colorful advertisement. They may want to use words from a provided word bank to add slogans or taglines. Students at this grade level may grasp only the most basic of concepts with relation to social and cultural context, so significant scaffolding in this area will be required. Concepts such as environmentally sound products as well as products that fit in our rapidly paced society are examples of ties that are familiar to younger students.

3rd Grade–5th Grade

Students at this age should be allowed to select a type of product of their choice and create an advertisement to share that product based on the principles learned from the activity (see Figure 19.1 on p. 142). A short discussion with the teacher can support the students in linking their product with the current historical era and tapping into areas of critical importance to society. For example, linking the sale of a piece of sports equipment might benefit from tying into a popular athlete or the Olympics.

6th Grade–8th Grade

Students at this age can learn about market competition as well as how different types of products are more desirable at different time periods in our history. Assign them the same type of item, but instruct them they will be advertising competing brands. Their job will be to come up with an advertisement that will sell their product more effectively than their competitors. At this grade level, they should make explicit ties to areas of societal interest as well as individual use of the product. Instruct students to leave off personal information from the final product and invite another classroom to view the advertisements. After viewing, ask the other students to indicate which product they are likely to try.

MEETING THE NEEDS OF ENGLISH LEARNERS

English learners may have difficulty understanding puns, metaphors, or other creative uses of language that might be a part of some advertisements. To support English learners with comprehension, select advertisements with straightforward slogans and language as well as images that closely align with the ad text.

MEETING THE NEEDS OF STUDENTS WITH SPECIAL NEEDS

The combination of images and text in advertisement analysis as well as creation of their original advertisement will support students who may have difficulty in the area of language arts. Students with limited fine motor abilities or with low vision may find the illustration of the original advertisement challenging. One modification to consider is to work with a peer or adult helper to create an advertisement through a magazine collage format.

ASSESSMENT SUGGESTION

At the conclusion of the activity, students will be able to:

- Analyze vintage advertisements
- Compare and contrast products of the past with those of the present
- Explore economic themes

Students' advertisements can serve as assessment pieces.

Score	Content Criteria	Presentation Criteria
4	Project contains detailed, clear information in all three areas: product description, benefits, and pricing information. Project has exceptional detail.	Project is very well organized, is neatly completed, and demonstrates the highest effort.
3	Project contains information in all three areas with basic detail.	Project is of acceptable quality.
2	Project contains information in two of the three areas.	Project lacks neatness and demonstrates a lack of organizational effort.
1	Project contains information in one or none of the three areas.	Project demonstrates minimal effort.

Children's Literature Connection

The Berenstain Bears and the Trouble With Commercials
By Jan and Mike Berenstain
ISBN: 0060573872
This book highlights how commercials can influence our purchasing and the importance of thinking critically in a manner suited for young children.

Quick Fact

Advertising involves more than influencing images and content information. Even the colors a company uses or the font they use for the company name has been carefully researched. Spend a minute thinking of your favorite stores. How does the way the company name is printed relate to the type of business it is?

FIGURE 19.1   Student Work Sample: Advertisement for the Oinky Bank (Molly, age 12)

REFERENCES

Marks, M., & Davis, C. (2006). Making the economic concept of scarcity oh-so-sweet: An activity for the K–12 classroom. *The Social Studies, 97*(6), 239–244.

National Council for the Social Studies. (1994). *Expectations of excellence: Curriculum standards for social studies.* Washington, DC: Author.

National Council of Teachers of English and International Reading Association. (1996). *Standards for the English language arts.* Urbana, IL: National Council of Teachers of English.

Symbolism and Social Studies

Strategy 20

The first-grade class sat quietly on the rug while the teacher shared images from different monuments. The Vietnam War Memorial, the Washington Monument, Mount Rushmore, and the small monument in their own town dedicated to the victims of September 11th. "What do all these pictures have in common?" Ms. Hoell asked the students.

"They're all for people who died," said Katya in a soft voice.

"You're right," answered Ms. Hoell. "But they are also for people who didn't die. These are monuments and memorials built to honor a very important event or time in history. They honor people who may have died during the event, but more important, they honor the event or time itself and everyone that it may have affected."

"My grandpa was in the Vietnam War," said Henry. "We went to that place in the picture last summer, and he got a little sad."

"Yes, monuments and memorials can sometimes make people emotional. They may feel sadness, pride, or even happiness. Do you remember what we have been studying in class?"

"Our town!" yelled the class together.

"You're right, we've been learning about our town. So we are going to create a monument for the founding of our town. Do you all remember the story about how our town was founded and how it got its name, 'Santa Monica?'"

"*Yes!*" yelled the class together again.

"Great, let's get to work brainstorming what a monument might look to honor the people who founded our city."

V isuals can be very important to students learning important content information. Sometimes the names and dates of important historical events are too abstract for students to commit to memory. When these events are tied to imagery and personal stories, however, the content becomes more relevant and thus easier to retain. Starting with local community sites that have great importance can be a great way to engage students in active learning (Morris, 2006) and can serve as preparation for exploring historic sites on a national or global scope.

Monuments are a type of memorial honoring an event, person, or special site (Dictionary.com Unabridged, n.d.) and can be found all over the world. Even the youngest students can comprehend the symbolism of a monument or other commemorative element (Morris, 2003). For many, a monument is a critical tie to an important event in history and a necessary reminder of the many lives affected by that event. It is not uncommon to have social scientists consult on monument projects. Large-scale events that touched many lives can be difficult to memorialize due to conflicting ideas of what an appropriate tribute would be. For events that might have been too far in the past for individuals to remember, historians might be called on to recall critical details about the event. For projects that honor a particular culture or ethnic group, members of that community as well as social scientists are often part of the team. This project will help students learn the many elements that go into planning a memorial or monument. By linking the assigned event to grade-level standards, the project can reinforce facts and figures of the event that might otherwise not be retained as well as promote critical-thinking skills (Martin, 2007). Although natural areas can also be identified as monuments (Dictionary.com Unabridged, n.d.), the focus of this activity will be manmade monuments or memorials such as plaques or statues erected to commemorate an event, person, or location.

Please visit www.sagepub.com/lmelberstudy for the updated National Council of the Social Studies standards.

Curriculum Standards for Social Studies

- Strand I: Culture
- Strand V: Individuals, Groups, & Institutions
- Strand X: Civic Ideals & Practices

Standards for the English Language Arts

As students work together in groups, they are not only developing the basics of linguistic fluency and vocabulary development but also how to communicate ideas clearly and with respect to dissenting opinions.

- Standard 4:   Students adjust their use of spoken, written, and visual language (e.g., conventions, style, vocabulary) to communicate effectively with a variety of audiences and for different purposes.

Technology Connection

Images of international, national, and local monuments and memorials can be located through a simple Internet search. Sharing student designs by posting them on a class Web site is a great way to share students' hard work.

Sources: National Council for the Social Studies, 1994; National Council of Teachers of English and International Reading Association, 1996.

KEY THEMES

Analyzing photographs

Interpreting historic events

Applying knowledge to decision making

MATERIALS

Images of monuments and memorials related to school curriculum

White drawing paper

Colored pencils/markers

PROCEDURES

Begin the activity by sharing images of recognizable monuments from around the United States. Examples on a national scope include:

- Washington Monument (Washington, DC)
- Mount Rushmore (South Dakota)
- Lincoln Memorial (Washington, DC)
- USS Arizona Memorial (Hawaii)
- National D-Day Memorial (Virginia)

However, it is likely that there are memorials or small-scale monuments in your own neighborhood. Images of both will be helpful for students. A discussion of symbolism will be important at this stage.

After reviewing the role of memorials and types of memorial structures or offerings, inform students they will be designing an original monument or other type of memorial in line with what is being studied in class. Options include assigning a particular event that students have been studying, such as travel along the Oregon Trail or the founding of their local community. Another option is for students to have the opportunity to select the event on their own.

Once the event or person has been selected, provide students with scrap paper and pencils to sketch and design their monument or other memorial (see Figure 20.1 on p. 147). Circulate and monitor students, offering support during this planning phase as needed. After students are satisfied with their plan, provide them with high-quality construction paper or drawing paper and colored pencils, markers, or crayons to create a final version of their design.

Set aside a place to display student images either in the classroom or on school grounds. Encourage students to add a short written description explaining the elements of their design and any symbolism that might be present.

GRADE-LEVEL MODIFICATION

K–2nd Grade

For these students, it can be helpful to focus on concrete, personally relevant events. Examples include recognizing the location of a special event, memorializing a favorite playground tree removed for construction, or creating a monument to an important community member. Highly controversial or tragic events such as September 11th, may be best reserved for students in older grades, who are better able to conceptualize multiple perspectives as well as deal objectively with sad or upsetting topics. However, for younger students already dealing with a community tragedy or loss, monument or memorial design may be a positive way to help students through a difficult period.

3rd Grade–5th Grade

Students at this age can benefit from focusing on creating monuments or memorials linked to themes and events in the standards. Content standards for these grade levels touch on important times and events in American history, but some curriculum programs do not adequately tap into the personal views, emotions, and experiences of individuals living during this time period. Monument or memorial design is one way to explore the human context surrounding these important events.

6th Grade–8th Grade

These students are often eager to assert opinions and explore how their opinions may be similar to or different from societal norms. Providing the opportunity to explore the process of memorializing controversial events as well as the importance of plural voices in the design of such memorials and monuments will be a good match for their interest level and social development.

ASSESSMENT SUGGESTION

At the conclusion of the activity, students will be able to:

- Analyze photographs and design of monuments and memorials
- Interpret historic events as they related to the design of a monument or memorial
- Apply knowledge to decision making in how best to design a monument or memorial

Students' final designs can be assessed using the following rubric:

Score	Content Criteria	Presentation Criteria
4	Exceptionally detailed design on monument or memorial, well tied to historical content.	Project is very well organized, is neatly completed, and demonstrates the highest effort.
3	Acceptably detailed design on monument or memorial, well tied to historical content.	Project is of acceptable quality.
2	Acceptably detailed design with some historical content errors.	Project lacks neatness and demonstrates a lack of organizational effort.
1	Minimally detailed design, or significant errors in historical content.	Project demonstrates minimal effort.

Children's Literature Connection

There is a wide selection of literature focused on specific monuments of the United States. A simple search will result in numerous title options. One series that may be helpful is the "Historic Monuments" series: Teaching & Learning Company, www.teachinglearning.com.

Quick Fact

Maya Lin was a senior in college when her design of a memorial for Vietnam War veterans was selected as the winning design through a national competition. Her youth, the fact she was a woman, as well as her Asian-American heritage are all noteworthy elements that made the selection of her design so inspiring to many Americans.

FIGURE 20.1   Sample Student Work

Monuments to personal interests and popular culture will be common among younger students without specific guidelines.

"Monument to the Comics: This monument has some of my favorite characters from comics. Comics really inspire me!" (Max, age 8)

REFERENCES

Dictionary.com Unabridged (v 1.1). (n.d.). *Monument.* Retrieved May 15, 2009, from http://dictionary.reference.com/browse/monument

Martin, L. A. (2007). The Monroe Doctrine: Critical thinking through the use of a commemorative coin. *The Social Studies, 98*(3), 93–98.

Morris, R. V. (2003). The nation's capital and first graders: A virtual trip to Washington, D.C. *The Social Studies, 94*(6), 265–269.

Morris, R. V. (2006). The land of hope: Third-grade students use a walking tour to explore their community. *The Social Studies, 97*(3), 129–132.

National Council for the Social Studies. (1994). *Expectations of excellence: Curriculum standards for social studies.* Washington, DC: Author.

National Council of Teachers of English and International Reading Association. (1996). *Standards for the English language arts.* Urbana, IL: National Council of Teachers of English.

UNIT V
Understanding Our World

A significant component of a quality social science curriculum is building awareness and understanding of global cultures (National Council for the Social Studies, 1994). As our student body becomes increasing culturally and linguistically diverse (Santamaria, 2009), not only is it critical to build an understanding about the world around us, but doing so in a manner that is both sensitive and supportive of students' own culture and traditions is imperative.

This unit will explore sharing global cultures with students in a manner that is both relevant and respectful. Emphasis on cultural universals such as music, currencies, and symbolism (Alleman, Knighton, & Brophy, 2007) allows students to explore similarities and differences among different cultures through a lens of personal relevance.

REFERENCES

Alleman, J., Knighton, B., & Brophy, J. (2007). Social studies: Incorporating all children using community and cultural universals as the centerpiece. *Journal of Learning Disabilities, 40,* 166–173.

National Council for the Social Studies. (1994). *Expectations of excellence: Curriculum standards for social studies.* Washington, DC: Author.

Santamaria, L. J. (2009). Culturally responsive differentiated instruction: Narrowing gaps between best pedagogical practices benefiting all learners. *Teachers College Record, 111*(1), 214–247.

Strategy
21

Connecting
to Music Studies

WORLD MUSIC

"Did you hear what Ms. Jones, our teacher, said about music?" asked Alyson.

"Yes, I did," commented Brian. "She said that children all over the world know about hip-hop and also sing songs from their own countries."

"To me that means that all children like the same music as we do, and I guess they have different music, too," concluded Alyson.

Parker (2009) contends that music, in its various forms of expression—singing, dancing, listening, and playing instruments—adds firsthand, hands-on experiences to social studies classrooms. These experiences add unforgettable meaning to social studies instruction as teachers find such melodies as folksongs that can be used to tantalize youngsters into learning about times and ways of life different than their own. In addition, Selwyn (1993) states that "music from different cultures can offer us an entry point to understanding people who may have lived thousands of years ago or thousands of miles from us" (p. 150).

Teachers can use music to help young students understand that it is through music that humans through the ages and still today express their deepest feelings. Using words, notes, rhythms, and movement, music transcends time and unites generations and cultures. Teaching children to sing songs from different times in the history of the nation has been a mainstay in many social studies classrooms. For example, the songs of the Civil Rights Movement, such as "We Shall Overcome," have been taught not only for their relevance to life and times in the 1960s but also for their reference to the sound and message of African American gospel and spiritual music. Helping students to learn about and appreciate cultures and people from other countries can also be facilitated by the use of music, and there are many resources to support this (Burton & McFarland, 2009).

Learners can be introduced to music as an aspect of social studies that can reveal much about a country's history, geography, and culture. Tracing the history of music's development in a specific country can lead to some surprising discoveries and cross-cultural connections. For example, if research is done on the troubadours—the roving singers of France—students will come to understand that this phenomenon was not unique to France. *Minnesingers* existed in Germany; *skalds* were singing in Scandinavia. The discovery of such similarities across cultures can lead to a class discussion that requires critical thinkers to make connections about why such singers traveled to deliver news and stories during this time period.

Opera too can be studied as a way to learn about specific countries and music that transcends cultures. Introducing learners to opera can be exciting as it is not what most students usually listen to. In addition to being taught to appreciate the beauty of the music of opera, the learners can be instructed about the historical events and legends that are the frequent subjects of this type of music. Introducing students to the music of Eastern cultures can also be most exciting because as with opera, its sounds are not those that most students frequently hear. For example, learners can come to understand that music from ancient China sounds different because the scale on which music was composed used a pentatonic (five-tone) scale in contrast to the octave (eight-tone) scale used in the West.

Students can come to appreciate the history and culture of the United States and other countries through music. They can also make personal connections as teachers challenge them to explore not only traditional but also contemporary music from around the world. However, much of the study of music in the social studies classroom should be fun.

Sources: National Council for the Social Studies, 1994; National Council of Teachers of English and International Reading Association, 1996.

Please visit www.sagepub.com/lmelberstudy for the updated National Council of the Social Studies standards.

Curriculum Standards for Social Studies

- Strand I: Culture
- Strand II: Time, Continuity, & Change
- Strand IV: Individual Development & Identity

Standards for the English Language Arts

This activity is a great way to explore written and oral communication strategies of other cultures and the role that song lyrics can play in communicating ideas that may be difficult to discuss.

- Standard 1:   Students read a wide range of print and nonprint texts to build an understanding of texts, of themselves, and of the cultures of the United States and the world; to acquire new information: to respond to the needs and demands of society and the workplace, and for personal fulfillment. Among these texts are fiction and nonfiction, classic and contemporary works.

- Standard 9:   Students develop an understanding of and respect for diversity in language use, patterns, and dialects across cultures, ethnic groups, geographic regions, and social roles.

Technology Connection

Video and audio will be central to this activity, providing students with firsthand experiences with different types of music. This National Geographic Web site can be a helpful resource for educators: http://worldmusic.nationalgeographic.com/worldmusic/view/page.basic/home.

KEY THEMES

Making observations

Finding patterns

Discussing to clarify ideas

Using technology to gather and organize data

Understanding the music's cross-cultural connections

MATERIALS (VARY ACCORDING TO TEACHER'S SELECTION OF ACTIVITIES LISTED ON BOARD)

Recordings of music from various cultures

Research materials/books/magazines/online sources

Videos of performances from various cultures

Instruments from various cultures

Music scores representing various cultures

PROCEDURES

The use of the choice or tic-tac-toe board strategy is one way for students to have fun with listening to, playing, researching, and understanding music from the United States and other countries. To construct a tic-tac-toe or choice board, select nine assignments that relate to the unit topic. In this case, the topic would be contemporary and traditional music around the world. Next, arrange these assignments in three rows and three columns—like a tic-tac-toe game board. The assignments can be arranged deliberately, such as all assignments in the first row have to do with listening, all in the second row have to do with researching, and all in the last row have to do with the production of music. The vertical columns can be used to indicate degree of difficulty with the first column containing the easiest work, the middle column having a moderate degree of difficulty, and the final column containing the most challenging assignments. Teachers can also choose to arrange assignments randomly on the board. If students are to complete assignments in the traditional manner of either vertical, horizontal, or perpendicular lines, then the board is called a tic-tac-toe board. If students are given more choices or different choices, such as being able to complete any three assignments on the board, the board is called a choice board (see box below).

Creating and Using a Choice Board

1. Column 1 requires relating to the actual traditional music of the country assigned. All activities demand speaking.
2. Column 2 requires relating to the national anthem of the country assigned. All activities require writing.
3. Column 3 asks learners to show the history of music, including contemporary music, in the country assigned. All activities require drawing or constructing.

---

4. Assignments in Row 1 are easiest, those in Row 2 are of normal difficulty, and those in Row 3 are the most difficult.

5. To complete the board, a student must do one activity from each row. They can select any activity from any column in this row. Such completion of the board will allow learners to choose from easy, normal, and most difficult assignments.

For assistance as they design these assignments, classroom teachers can and should turn to their music teacher colleagues. Such consultation will bring students to an understanding of the interdisciplinary connections among music, social studies, and all learning. Although this board activity is appropriate for students of any age, teachers should tailor what signifies completion of the activity based on student age. After individual students or groups have been assigned a specific country or region of the world, the entire board should be presented to the whole class and students instructed on how to complete the board. Questions that should be addressed include:

- Will students be required to complete the board as a tic-tac-toe?
- Will everyone have to complete the center square?
- Can learners comply by finishing certain rows or columns?
- How many boxes must be completed?
- Can additional boxes be completed for extra credit?

Once teachers decide and explain to the students how to complete the board, they explain each assignment and the assessment for each square.

Students should then be provided the materials—recordings, videos, Web sites, and so forth—to work on the assignment in each box and subsequently complete each assignment. It is most essential that teachers establish guidelines for the way students turn in completed work (see Figure 21.1 on p. 156).

- Will students hand in an assignment as soon as it is finished?
- Will students only hand in assignments when they have completed three according to teachers' directions?

Teachers also need to provide ways for learners to stay organized during this activity. Much differentiated work is going on with learners on different assignments and in various stages of completion. Folders for work in progress as well as completed assignments can be given. Teachers can extend this activity to include a reflective written piece by students. Students can be asked to comment on why they chose certain assignments and not others and also if they enjoyed the entire choice-board activity.

GRADE-LEVEL MODIFICATIONS

K–2nd Grade

It is essential that teachers ascertain whether these young learners know how to play tic-tac-toe. First they should be taught to play the game in the traditional way with Xs and Os. Teachers can model with the whole class and then allow students to play each other in pairs or teams. Understanding of the requirements for completion of each activity should then be determined. To make the selection of the assignments on the board more manageable for these young learners, some teachers may have the class as a whole select which boxes will be completed. In other words, after hearing about what each box means, the class discusses what is required and then decides which three box assignments they will complete, and everyone does the same assignments.

3rd Grade–5th Grade

Because directions for this activity are somewhat complicated, teachers should be sure that learners understand what is required. After teachers' explanation, students would benefit from being required to restate the directions and requirements either orally or in writing. Tailoring the assignment so that the requirements are very specific also provides task clarity. Assigning students to complete the choice board in pairs is appropriate at this age level. Such pairing allows the learners to clarify expectations and requirements for each other. A variation for completion of the assignments using pairs of students is having each student complete one box and then the pair completes the third box together.

6th Grade–8th Grade

Students at this age level particularly enjoy the idea of having a choice of which assignments to complete. Such choice promotes personal ownership, with students frequently working harder and better to reach personal and teacher expectations. Teachers can assign two or more students to investigate music from the same country. Then they could do a joint presentation of their choice-board answers so that the learning would be rich and complete for the entire class. Asking students to reflect on their assignment choices and the completion of the choice board is particularly important and successful at this age level. These learners like to think about their own thinking (metacognition) and like to explain the reasons for their actions to others.

MEETING THE NEEDS OF ENGLISH LEARNERS

The use of the choice board will support English learners, as they can select which assignments they feel secure and comfortable completing. The assignments, such as singing and playing instruments, are also designed to transcend language barriers. These students can be given the choice along with the rest of the class of whether to study about music from country of their origin or music from another country.

MEETING THE NEEDS OF STUDENTS WITH SPECIAL NEEDS

The choice board or tic-tac-toe activity is a mainstay of differentiated instruction. The assignments on the board can be customized to celebrate each learner's uniqueness and abilities. For example, for students with auditory difficulties or hearing loss, the board can be adapted to include more assignments about dance and the visual arts. Some teachers even tailor all the board's assignments and create individual boards that look like everyone else's yet are specially designed for learners with learning or communication disabilities.

ASSESSMENT SUGGESTION

At the conclusion of the activity, students will be able to:

- Recognize and speak about music from another country
- Contrast traditional and contemporary music from the United States and other countries
- Understand the significance of music to culture

Students' completion of the tic-tac-toe or choice-board activity can be assessed using a simple rubric such as the following:

Score	Criteria
4	All assignments are complete, and board directions are followed with exceptional detail and creativity.
3	All assignments are complete, and board directions are followed.
2	Most of the assignments are complete, and board completion directions are followed.
1	Only one assignment is complete, and board completion directions are not followed.

Children's Literature Connection

Children Just Like Me: Celebrations
  By Anabel Kindersley and Barnabas Kindersley
  ISBN: 0789420279
  This book, which is sponsored by UNICEF, details in words and pictures the celebrations and cultural traditions of children all over the world. Music is featured as an integral part of most celebrations and many traditions.

Hip Hop Around the World
  By Lindsey Sanna
  ISBN: 1422203506
  This volume traces the history of hip hop from the Bronx to its popularity today in Europe and Africa. The Jamaican roots of this music are also emphasized.

Quick Fact

The love of ancient Egyptians for things of colossal size is demonstrated in the large pyramids, sphinxes, and temples that were constructed. The orchestras of this time also were large. They sometimes had as many as six hundred players of harps, lyres, lutes, pipes, and mental rattles. Trumpets and tambourines were only used in the army.

| **FIGURE 21.1** | Connecting to Traditional and Contemporary Music Around the World Sample Choice or Tic-Tac-Toe Board | K–2nd, 3rd–5th, 6th–8th |

What country or region of the world are you investigating? _____

Listen to traditional music from the country you were assigned. Tell the class three things that you noticed about the music. _____ _____	Listen to the national anthem of the country you were assigned. Write about how listening makes you feel. _____ _____	Draw or construct three story boards to explain the history of music in the country you were assigned. The last board must be about contemporary music. _____ _____
Sing or play a traditional song from the country you were assigned. Tell the class something about the history of the song. _____ _____	Listen to the national anthem of the country you were assigned. Obtain a translation of the words to this song, and write about how the words relate to the country. _____ _____	Draw or construct a timeline of the history of music in the country you were assigned. Be sure to extend the timeline to the present day. _____ _____
Play a traditional instrument from the country you were assigned. Tell the class something about the history of the instrument in your country. _____ _____	Listen to the national anthem of the country you were assigned. Compare the words and music to the words and music of "The Star Spangled Banner." Write an essay to explain the comparison. _____ _____	Construct a Venn diagram in which you compare and contrast the history of music in the country you were assigned to the history of music in the United States. Be sure to include contemporary comparisons. _____ _____

Sources you used:

_____

_____

_____

_____

REFERENCES

Burton, J. B., & McFarland, A. L. (2009). Multicultural resources. *General Music Today, 22*(2), 30–33.

National Council for the Social Studies. (1994). *Expectations of excellence: Curriculum standards for social studies.* Washington, DC: Author.

National Council of Teachers of English and International Reading Association. (1996). *Standards for the English language arts.* Urbana, IL: National Council of Teachers of English.

Parker, W. C. (2009). *Social studies in elementary education.* Upper Saddle River, NJ: Prentice Hall.

Selwyn, D. (1993). *Living history in the classroom: Integrative arts activities for making social studies meaningful.* Chicago: Zephyr.

Currency as a Primary Source

Strategy 22

EXPLORING FOREIGN CURRENCY

"I am just so confused," complained Brooke. "What is this funny-looking coin? It is the size of a penny, but it has a picture of a lady on it."

"Oh look! With my magnifying glass I can see that the writing says something about Canada," said Luke. "Where did this coin come from?"

"My dad brought it home for me from when he was in Canada," replied Jay. "Do you think I can use it to buy something?"

The concept of money is something even very young children know and "get." Somehow, they figure out that a certain amount of currency can be exchanged for something they want, like a candy bar or new toy. Coins become a valuable commodity to be saved in piggy banks and eagerly received from the tooth fairy. This fascination with coins, money, and currency can help teachers turn students into young historians as they learn about other people and cultures by physically examining a country's currency:

- What images are depicted?
- Are important people memorialized?
- Why are these people important in this country?
- What events are shown?
- Why were these events important to the country's history?
- Was the event shown important in United States history also?
- What kind of events and who are the people who are shown on coins and paper currency in the United States?
- How are these events and people similar to those events and people celebrated on money in other countries?

Individual student data charts as well as a class collaborative chart could be compiled to show the answers to these questions. Young learners love to use magnifying glasses to really study, examine, and compare the money of different countries. Older students can be asked to examine and study what attributes constitute "good" currency:

- How heavy can money be so that it is still portable?
- How easy is the currency to counterfeit?
- How large a supply is enough but not too much?

Furthermore, by studying currency, students develop as young economists who grasp and understand, in a rudimentary way, such concepts as supply and demand and exchange rates. In the primary grades, it is sufficient to teach simple exchange. How much of an item can be bought for a dollar? How much can be purchased for a peso? In grades four and beyond, the ideas of calculating exchange rates and purchasing power can lead to very natural interdisciplinary connections with mathematics instruction.

Parker (2009) contends that economic ideas should be presented in real-life situations so that the learning is relevant to students' lives. Setting up and using a classroom store is an activity that can be tailored to engage all elementary learners (Griffiths, 2001). These activities can be as complex as setting up a classroom market economy, complete with savings and loan mechanisms, or as simple as a barter system in which young learners trade coins from various countries for goods.

Please visit www.sagepub.com/lmelberstudy for the updated National Council of the Social Studies standards.

Curriculum Standards for Social Studies

- Strand I: Culture
- Strand VII: Production, Distribution, & Consumption

Standards for the English Language Arts

As students complete their data sheets, they are building writing skills as well as exploring new vocabulary. They are likely to be using print and Internet resources to identify the different types of currency they've been assigned and interpret the imagery on the currency.

- Standard 7:   Students conduct research on issues and interests by generating ideas and questions, and by posing problems. They gather, evaluate, synthesize data from a variety of sources (e.g., libraries, databases, computer networks, video) to communicate their discoveries in ways that suit their purpose and audience.

- Standard 9:   Students develop an understanding and respect for diversity in language use, patterns, and dialects across cultures, ethnic groups, geographic regions, and social roles.

Technology Connection

For the most up-to-date information on currency exchange rates, a Web site aligned with international finance will be the most helpful. One option is CNN Money: http://money.cnn.com/data/currencies/

Sources: National Council for the Social Studies, 1994; National Council of Teachers of English and International Reading Association, 1996.

KEY THEMES

Comparing and contrasting currency from different countries

Making observations

Drawing conclusions

Identifying patterns

Understanding the meaning of various economic terms

Reinforcing map-reading skills

MATERIALS

Coins or paper currency from the United States

Coins or paper currency from other countries

Articles that students can pretend to purchase

PROCEDURES

The procedure for this activity is dependent on student age and purpose of the activity. Basically, the teacher obtains and provides money from the United States and other countries. Also, for younger students, the teacher can provide objects that the students can pretend to purchase with the money given to them. The classroom store can be a whole-class activity or set up as a learning station to be used at different times during social studies or mathematics instruction. Learning stations can be used to promote mutual inquiry and decision making as classmates can be assigned to complete the store station activities as pairs or in a cooperative group. Students will first be asked to examine the money and make some conclusions. Magnifying glasses can be used. The teacher should provide questions to direct the inquiry. Questions can relate to physical descriptions concerning the size, shape, and weight of the money as well as to what is depicted on the currency. Further questioning and discussion should concentrate on assisting young historians comparing the currencies from other countries to that of the money from the country they are most familiar with, the United States. The teacher can identify or have students identify on a world map the countries represented by the money.

Learners should then proceed to the class store or learning station store. Here they will be directed to use their currency to purchase items. Some teachers might actually have students use the money they were given to really purchase such items as papers, erasers, and pencils that can be used in the classroom. At the youngest grades, it is most appropriate for the teacher to be the storekeeper. Items also should be priced so that no change needs to be made. For example, a pencil could cost five cents or three pesos. With older students, a classmate can serve as storekeeper to set the price of items, conduct the bartering, and make change. This can be quite a challenge relating to the currency of other countries. However the activity is conducted, it is important that the teacher lead a concluding discussion to help learners draw conclusions comparing and contrasting currency, which leads to comparing and contrasting of countries.

GRADE-LEVEL MODIFICATIONS

K–2nd Grade

This age group will be most anxious to study the physical aspects of the coins and paper money. Historical facts about the people and items contained on the currency can be explained to teach these young historians particularly about Presidents Washington and Lincoln. Moving from the physical examination of money to using it to barter or purchase items is next. The teacher can model how to purchase using U.S. coins first and then using other currencies. Items should first be marked with prices in cents or dollars and then re-marked with the amount of foreign currency. The physical symbols for money ($, etc.) need to be explained before students make purchases. The sample data sheet directs these young economists to draw and make conclusions about their purchases (see Figure 22.1 on p. 162).

3rd Grade–5th Grade

These students might be less interested in the physical aspects of currency than younger learners. However, they might be asked to consider and learn about how it was decided who and what was pictured on currency. Students could be divided into cooperative groups to study the history of the penny, dime, dollar, peso, euro, and so forth. Each group then will present their findings to the class, and general conclusions can be reached about how and why different images are included on various currencies. The store activity can, as in the kindergarten to second-grade level, be used so students can purchase items with the money from the United States and other countries. The concept of an exchange rate can be introduced with results recorded on a comparison and contrast data sheet to answer such questions as:

1. One euro is worth $1.25. How much did you pay for the item you purchased in dollars? How much did you pay in euros?

2. It took you two Canadian dollars to buy the item you purchased. How much would this article cost in U.S. dollars?

(The teacher or students could check the daily exchange rate on the Internet to determine the exchange rate most accurately.)

6th Grade–8th Grade

These older learners might also benefit from physically examining currencies and relating images to famous people or events. They can use currency images as a springboard for focusing research papers and projects. The store activity can, as in the other grade levels, can be used to purchase items with money from the United States and other countries. Just as it was suggested for third to fifth graders, this activity can lead to comparisons of exchange rates. Other vocabulary terms relating to economics, such as *scarcity* and *supply and demand,* can be introduced and then applied to the store activity. Following a model like that suggested by Richmond (1973), the classroom role playing can be expanded to create a classroom marketplace with borrowing and issuing of credit or even a classroom society with banking, schooling, and manufacturing. In addition, students can use the Internet to shop virtually in the United States and other countries. The teacher can lead a discussion about how Internet sites are alike and different, rates of taxation and shipping and handling, and the availability of products throughout the world.

Meeting the Needs of English Learners

Students who are from different countries may want to bring in samples of their country's money and play the role of an expert on this currency. Because singling out a student is not recommended, allowing all students to share foreign currency they may have from trips or family members leaves this opportunity open without spotlighting a single student. Students can present to their classmates not just facts about the money but also their own or their family's stories about shopping in another country. Learners also can be encouraged to bring in pictures, if they have them, of stores and shopping. Pictures can also be shared from the Internet, and discussion can revolve around comparing and contrasting shopping in the United States with other countries. Parents should be assured that the money will be returned. A word bank or word wall with relevant terms will assist students in learning names for various countries' money and relevant economic terms.

Meeting the Needs of Students With Special Needs

Kinesthetic activity is provided by both examining the coins and physically being involved in the purchasing of the items. More time to complete the shopping experience can be given to support students who may have difficulties with mathematical computation. A visual aid diagram can be used to direct student movement and participation.

Assessment Suggestion

At the conclusion of this activity, students will be able to:

• Make observations about the physical aspects of and images contained on currency
• Use money from various countries to purchase items
• Compare and contrast customs and purchasing power in different countries

Students' data sheets can be assessed using a simple rubric such as the following:

Score	Criteria
4	All sections of data sheet are complete with exceptional detail and insight.
3	All sections are complete with an acceptable level of detail.
2	Most of the sections are complete with an acceptable amount of detail, or all sections are complete with significant errors.
1	Few of the sections are complete, or multiple errors are present.

Children's Literature Connection

Money (DK Eyewitness Books)
By Joe Cribb
ISBN: 0756613892
This book provides photographs of both modern and ancient money. In addition, students would be interested in the stories related to the use of money in different cultures and in different time periods.

Funny Money

By Florence Temko

ISBN: 1581960379

This book is fun. Students learn trivia about U.S. money, and they are also challenged to complete puzzles, understand jokes, and fold currency.

The Berenstain Bears' Trouble With Money

By Stan Berenstain and Jan Berenstain

ISBN: 0394859170

The Berenstain Bears are a favorite of all elementary students. In this book, Brother and Sister Bear come to find out the true meaning of money.

When the Bees Fly Home

By Andrea Cheng and Joline McFadden

ISBN: 0884482383

This book details a family's attempt to make money after the bees they raise stop making honey. Beyond this economic concept, it is a family story about a father-and-son relationship and can even be used to connect with science learning about bees and insects.

Quick Fact

The first U.S. coin was a one-cent piece minted in 1787. It had 13 links as part of its image. These links represented the 13 original states.

Massachusetts issued paper money to pay its troops in 1690. This is the earliest evidence of the issue of paper money in what became the United States.

FIGURE 22.1   Exploring Money Sample Data Sheet   K–2nd Grade

Draw a picture of the U.S. money:

Draw a picture of the money from another country:

How are they alike?

_____

_____

_____

_____

How are they different?

_____

_____

_____

_____

What could you buy with your money?

_____

_____

_____

_____

How did you feel using the different types of money?

_____

_____

_____

_____

REFERENCES

Griffiths, R. (2001). Money and shops, role play and real life. *Mathematics Teaching, 174,* 20–22.

National Council for the Social Studies. (1994). *Expectations of excellence: Curriculum standards for social studies.* Washington, DC: Author.

National Council of Teachers of English and International Reading Association. (1996). *Standards for the English language arts.* Urbana, IL: National Council of Teachers of English.

Parker, W. C. (2009). *Social studies in elementary education.* Upper Saddle River, NJ: Prentice Hall.

Richmond, G. H. (1973). *The micro-society school: A real world in miniature.* New York: Harper and Row.

Strategy
23

Stamps as
Primary Sources

STORIES THAT STAMPS TELL

"My mother took me to the post office yesterday, and on the walls, there were pictures of all kinds of stamps," commented Alton. "I thought that stamps went on letters so that they could travel to other people. What were those pictures?" he continued.

"I think it means there are many different stamps," Lorelei responded. "I have a question, too. In other countries, do they use stamps to get letters from one place to another?"

"I think they do, because my father has books that he uses to collect stamps from all over the world," responded Joey.

Stamps are a common household item to most of even the very youngest elementary school children. They see them on letters delivered by the mail carrier. They see their parents stick them on correspondence to be sent to others. Teachers can use this firsthand experience and background knowledge to springboard into studying history and the reading of biographies (Mealy & Schneider, 1981). They can provide learners with opportunities to compare and contrast the images and people featured on stamps not only from the United States but also from countries around the world.

For younger students, teachers can continue to provide lessons that help these learners understand their neighborhood, including a trip to the post office or a visit to the classroom by a mail carrier. During these experiences, questions can also be raised about how to buy and use stamps as well as the purpose of using them.

Stamps can be studied as primary source documents for the time when they were issued. Why were certain events or people memorialized at this time in history? For example, in 2009, four commemorative stamps were issued to honor the 100th birthday of President Abraham Lincoln. These four stamps provide a chronological look at Lincoln's life as they present him as rail splitter, lawyer, politician, and president. Students, even in the earliest grades, could be asked to do research relating to one of these aspects of Lincoln's life. There are many excellent biographies of this president available as picture books. After the learners have completed their individual research, they can each be asked to present their findings in chronological order. This cooperative learning jigsaw activity can give all class members a complete view of Abraham Lincoln's life and times. Teachers can expand this study of Lincoln by explaining that since 1866, this president has been featured on 74 stamps. These stamps can be viewed on the Smithsonian's National Post Office Museum Web site: http://arago.si.edu. This activity can be expanded to include stamps from other countries. For example, students can examine Canadian stamps and learn how many times Queen Elizabeth has been depicted.

Using the portraits and images on stamps as the starting point to read biographies and study about the historical figures and events is an activity that can be used in all elementary classrooms. This activity can include not only studying about important events and people in U.S. history but also about events and people from other parts of the world. Furthermore, students can be challenged to compare and contrast by researching and reading about stamp images from the United States and other countries. Older students can be asked to research or study subjects who appear on stamps of two different countries. They could be asked to study a specific year and contrast what stamps were issued in various countries during this time.

Sources: National Council for the Social Studies, 1994; National Council of Teachers of English and International Reading Association, 1996.

Please visit www.sagepub.com/lmelberstudy for the updated National Council of the Social Studies standards.

Curriculum Standards for Social Studies

- Strand I: Culture
- Strand II: Time, Continuity, & Change
- Strand III: People, Places, & Environments

Standards for the English Language Arts

Students are building research skills as they delve into the history of stamps. Completing their data sheets builds writing skills and their ability to summarize key themes and ideas.

- Standard 1:   Students read a wide range of print and nonprint texts to build an understanding of texts, of themselves, and of the cultures of the United States and the world; to acquire new information; to respond to the needs and demands of society and the workplace; and for personal fulfillment. Among these texts are fiction and nonfiction, classic and contemporary works.

- Standard 7:   Students conduct research on issues and interests by generating ideas and questions, and by posing problems. They gather, evaluate, and synthesize data from a variety of sources (e.g., print and nonprint texts, artifacts, people) to communicate their discoveries in ways that suit their purpose and audience.

Technology Connection

The U.S. Postal Service Web site is a great place for students to see images of currently circulating stamps as well as learn more about postage rates and even stamp collecting: www.usps.gov.

KEY THEMES

Comparing and contrasting

Making inferences

Drawing conclusions

Reading for factual content

Researching using diverse sources

Reinforcing map-reading skills

Writing and reporting

MATERIALS

Stamps from the United States

Stamps from other countries

Biographies, autobiographies, historical fiction relating to the people and events depicted on the stamps

Data sheet

PROCEDURES

The purpose of this activity is to have students of all grade levels develop an appreciation not only of U.S. history but also of the history of other countries through the examination of postal stamps. Basically, the teacher obtains postage stamps from the United States and other countries. Students then complete a data sheet that leads them to answer questions about the person or event depicted (see Figure 23.1 on p. 169). The answers to these questions can be found either in group or individual research. The teacher needs to work with the school media specialist to determine appropriate texts with regard to the students' grade and reading levels. Texts can include more than encyclopedias, Web sites, and general reference works. Biographies, autobiographies, nonfiction texts, and historical fiction can be used to enhance understanding. Students can be challenged to uncover the storyline in each of these types of texts. Uncovering this narrative will help them better relate to and understand people and times past.

This activity can be tailored to each grade level through the use of a K-W-L—Know, Want to Know, and Learned—chart, which requires students to individually list what they already know in the "K" column. In the "W" column, they list what they would like to learn, which should direct their research. The "L" column is where students list what they learned by studying and researching the person or events depicted on the stamp or stamps they investigated.

The selection of which stamps to be studied is important, as the teacher can collect those that are most relevant to the school's curriculum. Also, it is important for the teacher to consider that he or she could, at some grade levels, be asking learners to compare and contrast stamps from different countries; therefore, the subjects on the selected stamps need to be compatible.

The teacher will begin by leading a general discussion about the purpose of postal stamps. Students can contribute by talking about what they already know about stamps and the post office, or the teacher can direct them to fill out the "K" column on their

K-W-L chart. Next, the teacher gives each student a stamp or stamps to examine. The students follow the data chart's questions to answer who or what the stamp depicts. Then the students are directed to begin their research by doing general reading about the stamp image. The students will select additional print sources—biographies, autobiographies, nonfiction, and so forth—to complete their research. Younger students can be assessed by examining what information they record on the data sheet. Older students can be required to use the data sheet as an outline for the completion of a research report.

GRADE-LEVEL MODIFICATIONS

K–2nd Grade

This age group will be anxious to orally share with their teacher what they already know about stamps, letters, and the post office. The teacher can create a "what we know" chart on large paper to record each learner's prior knowledge. Then, the class can fill out a "what we want to learn about stamps" chart. Both of these charts can be used to anchor future learning. For this age group, the teacher may want to place the stamps to be examined into plastic sleeves to prevent them from being lost or damaged. Also, instead of each student doing a comparison of stamps from the United States and those from another country, the class could be divided into two groups. Half would examine U.S. stamps, and the other half would look at foreign stamps. The teacher would facilitate the comparisons. Finally, letting the students work in pairs or groups will provide collaborative activity that might facilitate quality completion of the data sheet.

3rd Grade–5th Grade

This age group would complete the K-W-L chart individually, with the teacher collating the results based on a discussion by the whole group. Students are capable to doing a comparison and contrast not only of the stamps but of the people and events pictured on them. The teacher would decide the format for the products of the learners' research; for example, students could be asked to report orally, write a report, or do both. The research process would be directed by the questions on the data chart. As an extension activity, learners could be asked to design and produce a stamp that represents themselves or an event in their lives that was significant. These stamps echo the U.S. Post Office's product that allows individuals to put images on postal stamps.

6th Grade–8th Grade

These older learners would complete the K-W-L chart individually, with the teacher collating the results based on a whole-group discussion. Students complete the data chart to direct their research. The teacher could decide how students will report their research, or the teacher could give learners the option of choosing between either presenting orally or writing a report. In addition, the project can be expanded to require students to read at least one book of historical fiction about topic portrayed by either of their stamps. They would next evaluate how accurate the historical fiction was compared to historical accounts. As an extension activity, students could be asked to design and produce a stamp that represents their school. This activity replicates the U.S. Post Office's product that allows creation of personal stamps.

MEETING THE NEEDS OF ENGLISH LEARNERS

Students who are from different countries may want to bring in stamps from their country, which makes them an active part of the classroom activities. Learners can then speak about these stamps or about how they received the stamps. Do people and relatives from the country write to them or their families? How long does it take to correspond back and forth? Pairing the English learner with another student to complete the data sheet as a comparison and contrast will help both learners. These modifications for meeting the needs of English learners should be used by the teacher with caution. The intent is not to single out any learner but rather to celebrate the diversity of students' experiences.

MEETING THE NEEDS OF STUDENTS WITH SPECIAL NEEDS

To meet the needs of students with disabilities, the teacher needs to consider ways to differentiate this lesson and the accompanying activity. With regard to content and process, the data sheets can be completed as a collaborative effort among a group of students. With regard to product and assessment, the teacher could require the same final product, but in assessing, give different weighted values to support the achievement of each learner.

ASSESSMENT SUGGESTION

At the conclusion of this activity, students will be able to:

- Read for factual knowledge about historical events and people not only in and from the United States but also in and from other parts of the world
- Analyze and synthesize information from multiple sources, including nonfiction and fiction
- Compare and contrast historical events and famous people

Students' data sheets can be assessed using a simple rubric such as the following:

Score	Criteria
4	All sections of data sheet are complete with exceptional detail and insight.
3	All sections are complete with an acceptable level of detail.
2	Most of the sections are complete with an acceptable amount of detail, or all sections are completed with significant errors.
1	Few of the sections are complete, or multiple errors are present.

Children's Literature Connection

The Postage Stamp
By Jennifer Fandel
ISBN: 1583415548
This richly illustrated book is full of pictures of stamps from around the world. The history of stamps is detailed in a timeline.

Quick Fact

Only two famous Americans were featured on U.S. regular-issue stamps from 1908 through 1919: George Washington and Benjamin Franklin. A stamp was also created by the astronauts during the Apollo 11 moon landing in 1969. The astronauts made an impression of the moon's surface with a stamp die. When they returned to earth, the die was used to create an airmail stamp.

FIGURE 23.1 Exploring Stamps Sample Data Sheet · · · · · · · · · · · 3rd–5th

Stamp A:
Draw a picture of the U.S. stamp that you were given.

Who or what is shown on the stamp?

_____

_____

_____

When was this stamp issued? _____

Why do you think the person or event shown on this stamp is important?

_____

_____

_____

How did you find out about the person or event on this stamp? (What book, magazine, or Web site did you use?)

_____

Whom did you talk to about this?

_____

_____

Stamp B:
Draw a picture of the U.S. stamp that you were given.

(Continued)

FIGURE 23.1 (Continued)   3rd–5th

Who or what is shown on the stamp?

_____

_____

_____

When was this stamp issued? _____
Why do you think the person or event shown on this stamp is important?

_____

_____

_____

How did you find out about the person or event on this stamp? (What book, magazine, or Web site did you use?)

_____

Whom did you talk to about this?

_____

_____

Comparing Stamps A and B:
How are these stamps alike?

_____

_____

_____

How are they different?

_____

_____

_____

REFERENCES

Mealy, V. T., & Schneider, J. (1981) It's a sticky business . . . but for students, stamp collecting is a first class idea. *Instructor, 90*(6), 66–69.

National Council for the Social Studies. (1994). *Expectations of excellence: Curriculum standards for social studies.* Washington, DC: Author.

National Council of Teachers of English and International Reading Association. (1996). *Standards for the English language arts.* Urbana, IL: National Council of Teachers of English.

Understanding Global Symbols

ANALYSIS OF FLAG SYMBOLISM

"Hey, Jose, did you ever think about how many places you can see our country's flag?" asked Jessica.

"What do you mean?" answered Jose.

"Well, we see it every day outside our school. The flag hangs in our classroom and in all the others. I see it when I go to the post office with my mom. I even see the American flag flying at my grandpa's house," said Jessica.

"Gee, I never thought of that," Jose responded. "I wonder if it is the same in Mexico where my family comes from. I wonder what their flag looks like."

Even the very youngest of students has seen flags displayed on public buildings, in classrooms, and on homes. In addition, they often have seen a variety of flags—American flags, state flags, prisoner of war flags, and so forth. However, very young learners have generally not thought about or been taught about the flag as a symbol. In particular, they may not realize that the flag of each country is not merely a piece of cloth made of colors and images. Rather, this flag is the chief symbol or representation of the country. Teachers of younger students may have more difficulty helping their students deal with this level of abstraction. It will take patience to explain why the flag is a piece of cloth but is much more than just the material from which it is made. The flag of any country stands for its country, its people, its government, and its ideals. Parker (2009) extols social studies teachers of young learners to be patient as they teach the abstract idea of symbolism.

Connecting the idea of a physical flag to the ideals, nation, and people it symbolizes can begin with a look at the current American flag. Teachers and students at all elementary levels can examine the colors, placement of these colors, and the images of lines and stars. Such as examination can help students activate prior knowledge not only about our flag's history but also about design and the use of certain colors. It would be interesting to share with the class that the Congress in 1777 adopted a resolution that a red, white, and blue flag should be made to symbolize the unity and independence of the United States. However, no one really knows why the colors were chosen. In 1782, the Department of State declared the colors to have the following meanings: red represents hardiness and courage, white symbolizes purity and innocence, and blue stands for vigilance, perseverance, and justice. Once students have examined and discussed the flag, the teacher can lead them to consider how seeing the flag makes them feel. Do they feel safe when they see it flying in front of their school? Do they feel proud that such a beautiful flag represents the United States? Students could be asked to talk about the American flag and what it means with their parents, grandparents, and other family members. Some might hear poignant stories about flags at citizenship ceremonies, the funerals of presidents and soldiers, or other historical events. These stories can help cement in a learner's mind that a flag is much more than itself. It is representative of people and nations.

Teachers could also have students examine and talk about their state flags. All state flags can be discussed not only in relation to the colors selected and how they make the viewer feel but also in relation to the images contained on the flag. Looking at, analyzing, and explaining these images will provide background knowledge for when the learners look at the flags of other countries. To begin the discussion of flags of other countries and their symbolism, teachers can select the flag of a country that the class has been studying or will study and conduct the same kind of discussion as to colors used, images portrayed, and symbolic meaning. Actual flags or pictures of flags obtained from the Internet or the myriad books on flags can be used for any or all of these activities.

Having students create a page for a class alphabet book of flags from various countries gets them involved in a personal way as an expert on that nation and its flag. The creation of this book as a jigsaw cooperative learning activity creates a classroom community that can then engage in conversation comparing and contrasting the flags and the countries with each other and also with the American flag and nation. First, each learner can talk about his or her page and the flag and country shown. Once all students have presented their pages, discussion to compare and contrast flag colors and symbols can ensue.

Please visit www.sagepub.com/lmelberstudy for the updated National Council of the Social Studies standards.

Curriculum Standards for Social Studies

- Strand I: Culture
- Strand III: People, Places, & Environment
- Strand X: Civic Ideals & Practices

Standards for the English Language Arts

Students will be developing their research skills as they explore the history and design of different flags. Capturing their discoveries and sharing them orally or through writing also taps into critical language arts skills.

- Standard 4:   Students adjust their use of spoken, written, and visual language (e.g., conventions, style, vocabulary) to communicate effectively with a variety of audiences and for different purposes.

Sources: National Council for the Social Studies, 1994; National Council of Teachers of English and International Reading Association, 1996.

- Standard 8: Students use a variety of technological and informational resources (e.g., libraries, databases, computer networks, video) to gather and synthesize information and to create and communicate knowledge.

- Standard 9: Students develop an understanding of and respect for diversity in language use, patterns, and dialects across cultures, ethnic groups, geographic regions, and social roles.

- Standard 10: Students whose first language is not English make use of their first language to develop a competency in the English language arts and to develop understanding of content across the curriculum.

Technology Connection

Students may want to explore the use of a computer-based drawing program to design a flag to represent their family, the classroom, or the school.

KEY THEMES

Making observations

Identifying patterns

Questioning

Discussing to clarify ideas

Using technology to gather data

Comparing and contrasting flags as symbols of different nations

MATERIALS

Flags or pictures of flags from countries other than the United States

Paper (heavy duty) to be used for pages of book

Craft materials (selected by teacher and students): markers, construction paper, glue, glitter, stickers, and so forth

Reference resources for older students

PROCEDURES

The procedure for this activity is the same for all elementary students no matter what grade they are. Learners will create a page for a class book on flags of different countries. The teacher will assign a flag and country or perhaps the students can select a flag and country based on their interests, knowledge, or family origin. The teacher will provide a template of what a page should look like (see Figure 24.1 on p. 177). Some like the students to complete their page based on a very specific template with, for example, the size and placement of the beginning letter to be placed in the upper right-hand corner of the page. Other specifications can include where the name of the country is placed and how large the depicted flag should be. Other teachers allow the students more creative leeway and consider the page a success if it contains the letter, country name, and flag in any arrangement.

Once the teacher has decided on the "look" of the pages of the book, modeling the process for completing individual pages is essential. The teacher should create a sample page in front of or with the class. The look of the page depends on the specifications established by the teacher as determined by the grade level of the learners. Some pages will contain pasted pictures. Other might contain flags students have constructed from colored paper. Some teachers set no specifications as to the construction of the flag on each page and give individual students the choice to cut out pictures, draw flags, or construct them from various materials, such as cloth, paper, and so on.

To complete the book, the pages are alphabetized and the book is bound together. No matter how the pages are put together (binding machine, staples, etc.), the teacher must be proactive and warn the learners not to write or draw to the ends of the paper.

GRADE-LEVEL MODIFICATIONS

K–2nd Grade

This age group can be given larger paper on which to compose their book. A classroom book on chart paper might permit young learners to be more comfortable, expressive, and creative. Teachers can also write the letter and name of the country on each learner's paper with the student's responsibility being to depict the flag. Students can paste a picture, draw a picture, or make the flag out of construction paper, depending on teachers' directions. An option to creating a big book of flags is for the teacher to use standard size or a little larger paper for each page and to print the alphabet letter and country name on each before giving pages to students. A space for the flag depiction can also be indicated. Also, countries selected for the flag pages for this age group can be narrowed to a specific continent or region. Once all pages have been completed, teachers can have the class alphabetize the pages as a group before they are bound together. The completed book can be used as a teacher read-aloud to promote comparison and contrast discussion. The book can become part of the classroom library.

3rd Grade–5th Grade

It is essential that teachers clearly explain the parameters of the assignment. Each learner will create his or her own page that contains the alphabet letter of the first name of the country, the country name, and the flag. Page and component sizes can be specified by teachers or left to the student's creativity. Additional information, such as size, location, geography, and important historical events can be required about the flag's country on each page (see Figure 24.2 on p. 178).

At this age level, some teachers have used this alphabet page book activity as a way to increase students' technological literacy. In other words, the computer and the Internet are the vehicles for the production of the book. Students are given a computer template that they fill in, and they cut and paste from Internet sources, use computer tools to draw, and do research online. The result is a uniform product—a book that is easy to follow because of the exact formatting on each page. Information from each page can then be readily accessed for comparison and contrast discussions. An extension activity could be for learners to design a flag to represent themselves—their ideals, hopes, dreams, and who they really are. These flags could be displayed in the classroom. Learners could also design these flags for a class alphabet book. Each page would be devoted to the learner with the beginning letter of the first name, full name, flag, and important facts.

6th Grade–8th Grade

Creating a page for an alphabet book might seem childish to this age group. Teachers need to establish criteria for the dimensions and look of each page. More important, they need to set expectations for the content of each page. The letter, country, and flag must be included. In addition, information about the country and even the history of the country's flag might be required. Therefore, each learner's section of the book could be more than a page. Students could work with traditional paper and craft materials, or they could produce a classroom book entirely on computer. If the classroom book is constructed on the computer, each learner can have his or her own copy. These individual copies can then be read prior to a comparison and contrast discussion. This preparation would lead not only to learners being responsible for the own pages but also to students asking questions of others about their work. An extension activity could be for learners, either as a whole class or in small groups, to design and create a flag to represent their school. If the whole class designs the flag, it and an explanation of how the flag represents the school can be presented to the principal. If small groups create various flags, the class could vote on which one the majority feels best represents the school and present that flag to the principal.

MEETING THE NEEDS OF ENGLISH LEARNERS

The direct teaching approach, with teachers setting parameters for the assignment and completion of pages, helps English learners complete the assignment successfully. Some English learners with limited language ability might want to create their page in their native language. The teacher can work with the learners to complete the page in English or have the learner use translation software to prepare a page that is comparable to other students' work.

MEETING THE NEEDS OF STUDENTS WITH SPECIAL NEEDS

The direct teaching and modeling approach, with teachers setting specific parameters for the look and content of the learner's page, is important for all learners, but these firm expectations might be daunting to some learners with disabilities. Teachers need to work with the strengths of each child but particularly those with disabilities. A student who has trouble writing due to either a physical or cognitive difficulty could explain the flag and its meaning to the class orally. Students who need to use assistive technology in the form of electronic readers or computers for writing should be provided such assistance.

Assessment Suggestion

At the end of this activity, students will be able to:

- Understand and state the relationship between the flag as a symbol and the nation it represents
- Analyze and synthesize information from multiple research sources
- Compare and contrast different flags and what they represent

Students' alphabet book flag pages can be assessed by using a simple rubric such as the following:

Score	Criteria
4	Page contains more than the required information. All sections of the page meet directions.
3	Page contains all required information. All sections of the page meet directions.
2	Most of the required information is contained on the page. Most of the directions for placement on page are followed.
1	Some of the required information is missing. Directions for placement of information on page are not followed.

Children's Literature Connection

Complete Flags of the World
   By DK Publishing
   ISBN: 0756641152
   This book can be a good resource for learning more about flags from countries around the world.

Quick Fact

Another name for the American flag is *Old Glory*. The story behind that name is quite fascinating. In 1831, William Driver was a sea captain who, for some unknown reason, decided to call the American flag flown on his ship *Old Glory*. Driver traveled around the world sporting the same flag, *Old Glory*, on all of his voyages. In 1837, he retired and took the flag with him to his home in Nashville, Tennessee. During the Civil War, Driver hid the flag by having it sewn into a bed quilt. In 1862, when Union troops arrived in Nashville, the flag was rescued and flew over the state capitol. This flag was given to the Smithsonian Institution in 1922.

FIGURE 24.1   Flags of the World Sample Alphabet Book Page   K–2nd Grade

C
Canada

FIGURE 24.2 Flag Analysis Sample Data Sheet   3rd–5th, 6th–8th

Country: _____

Image of flag:

Facts about this country:

_____

_____

_____

_____

_____

Observations about this country's flag:

_____

_____

_____

_____

_____

What about the flag connects to what you know about the country?

_____

_____

_____

_____

_____

REFERENCES

National Council for the Social Studies. (1994). *Expectations of excellence: Curriculum standards for social studies*. Washington, DC: Author.

National Council of Teachers of English and International Reading Association. (1996). *Standards for the English language arts*. Urbana, IL: National Council of Teachers of English.

Parker, W. C. (2009). *Social studies in elementary education*. Upper Saddle River, NJ: Prentice Hall.

Strategy 25

Authentic Geography and Cartography Studies

WHERE IN THE WORLD?

"My grandma said that the street where I live used to be called Butler Street when she was a little girl," complained Rosemary. "I just don't get it," she continued, "I live on Taylor Road. Do the names of streets change?"

"Not only do the names of streets change, but my Grandpa told me that sometimes the names of countries even change," commented Jacob. "He says when he was a little boy he lived in Czechoslovakia, and now, his hometown is in the Czech Republic."

"If we look at a map, we could find out what the names of streets and countries are today," said Juanita, "but I wonder how we can find out what streets and countries were called in the past?"

◆

To teach students geography is to teach them to study space and place on the earth. Maps are an important tool to assist learners, as they represent the world in spatial terms (Ekiss, Trapido-Lurie, Phillips, & Hinde, 2007). However, because the earth is really a sphere, maps are always somewhat distorted flat pictures of the three-dimensional earth. Try as they might, cartographers through the ages, from Mercator in the 1500s to Fuller in the 1960s, could not seem to eliminate the distortions. Nevertheless, maps have been essential navigation tools that help humans get from one place to another. Maps also can be viewed as historical documents that reflect the time, place, and knowledge available at their creation. Comparing historic and modern world maps can provide students with much to learn and to discuss, for example, about changes in country names and borders and the reasons for these changes.

In order for learners to begin to look at maps and see what they represent, it is essential for teachers to instruct them on how to read maps. Maps are complex pictures that require learners as readers and interpreters to master a variety of skills. They must know about map scale and map symbols to locate places. Once learners know about scale and symbols, they proceed to interpreting what is on the maps. This activity asks learners to make a cursory examination of maps of the same place from two different time periods. The purpose of this activity is not to create mini-cartographers but rather to foster critical thinkers who can see how basic differences in maps can be interpreted. Such differences or changes can be seen as the result of political, social, or economic upheavals. Older elementary students can study the "whys" of these map changes. Younger elementary students can look at these map changes as part of their study of change as a constant in human life. Changes in maps can be compared with changes due to growth in themselves. This activity is basically to provide students with a vehicle to focus their ability to compare and contrast two objects.

Sources: National Council for the Social Studies, 1994; National Council of Teachers of English and International Reading Association, 1996.

Please visit www.sagepub.com/lmelberstudy for the updated National Council of the Social Studies standards.

Curriculum Standards for Social Studies

- Strand II :   Time, Continuity, & Change
- Strand III: People, Places, & Environment
- Strand VIII: Science, Technology, & Society

Standards for the English Language Arts

Students can build vocabulary as they learn about newly formed countries as well as countries whose names have changed.

- Standard 1:   Students read a wide range of print and nonprint texts to build an understanding of texts, of themselves, and of the cultures of the United States and the world; to acquire new information: to respond to the needs and demands of society and the workplace, and for personal fulfillment. Among these texts are fiction and nonfiction, classic and contemporary works.

- Standard 5:   Students employ a wide range of strategies as they write and use different writing process elements appropriately to communicate with different audiences for a variety of reasons.

- Standard 8:   Students use a variety of technological and informational resources (e.g., libraries, databases, computer networks, video) to gather and synthesize information and to create and communicate knowledge.

Technology Connection

The National Geographic Web site has a number of different elements related to maps and mapping you might find helpful: www.nationalgeographic.com/maps.

KEY THEMES

Making observations

Interpreting charts and maps

Finding patterns

Finding relationships

Inferring

Developing historical perspective

Writing to demonstrate ability to compare and contrast

MATERIALS

Maps of same area at different times in history

Data sheets

PROCEDURES

The purpose of this activity is to have learners of all ages develop their ability to compare and contrast visual images in the form of maps. Then, they write about what they have observed in each map and compare and contrast these findings. Teachers give students two maps of basically the same area. One is from the past; the other from today. Each map must be identified with a number or letter that correlates with the other map of the same area but of a different time. For example, assigning the older map the number 1 and the letter "a" and the newer map the number 1 and the letter "b" will alert the student to the facts that both maps are of the same area (number 1) but from different times (letters a and b). Learners fill out the data sheet as they look at and observe the features on each map (see Figure 25.1 on p. 184). Next, they note what is alike on the two maps. Then they return to their original lists of features on each map to complete the data chart by noting how the maps are different. Each age level can complete the procedure. The reporting of the findings will get increasingly complex as students get older.

GRADE-LEVEL MODIFICATIONS

K–2nd Grade

It is best for this age group that teachers simplify maps that are already available in print. For example, teachers can narrow what the students compare to a small area of a country or region of the world. Teachers can begin map study by having students construct maps of their own rooms or a room in their house. Then students can learn to compare and contrast by using the maps they created and comparing them to the maps of other learners. It is important that teachers limit the number of map symbols that young learners encounter. They sometimes have difficulty connecting the symbol with its meaning. In addition, some young learners have difficulty conceptualizing that maps are flat drawings of the three-dimensional world. Using the Internet, specifically Google Earth, to locate places they are familiar with, should help them understand better.

3rd Grade–5th Grade

Students should already have some familiarity with map reading by the time they are in Grades 3 through 5. It would be interesting to introduce students to the different types of maps—climate, transit, political, physical, resource, and elevation. In addition to completing the activity by asking them to compare and contrast maps from different time periods, they could be challenged to study two different types of maps of the same area.

The data sheet for this age group should be used as part of the prewriting step for composing a paragraph or essay comparing and contrasting the two maps.

6th Grade–8th Grade

Students should be acquainted with map-reading skills. The purpose of completing the data chart is to serve as a prewriting step to composing an essay. This essay should begin with an opening statement about the student's conclusions relating to comparing and contrasting the maps. The first paragraph should present details on the older map; the second details on the newer map. The third paragraph should stress how the maps are alike; the fourth how they are unlike. The final, concluding paragraph should contain some plausible explanation for the similarities and differences. Through this essay writing, students are demonstrating that they are acquiring historical perspective through the study of cartography. As an extension to this activity, a member of a historical group or society could be asked to bring maps from various eras to the class and talk to the students about changes in their own community.

MEETING THE NEEDS OF ENGLISH LEARNERS

English learners can orally describe each map and draw conclusions about similarities and differences between the time periods. Teachers can work with these learners as a group or individually to help them complete the data sheet. Teachers should listen carefully to the students talking about the maps and then record the answers on a large version of the data chart. After completing the chart, teachers can work with the learner or learners to create a group paragraph or essay. This paragraph or essay likewise can be written on large chart paper, and students can then use it as a model for writing their own paragraph or essay.

MEETING THE NEEDS OF STUDENTS WITH SPECIAL NEEDS

Teachers need to understand that the basic idea that students are to learn from this activity is that maps show us that names and borders change over time. Simplifying the data sheet so that it is completed as a jigsaw activity by a group of learners can facilitate understanding by those who have difficulty understanding the task. Some students with reading difficulties might find this activity easier than reading a textbook. Students with low vision can be given globes and maps that have raised features. Also, maps obtained from Internet sources can be enlarged easily through the use of projection equipment, which will make the maps and their features easier to distinguish.

ASSESSMENT SUGGESTION

Students' preliminary data charts can be assessed by using a simple rubric such as the following:

Score	Criteria
4	All sections of the data sheet are complete with exceptional detail and insight.
3	All sections of the data sheet are complete with an acceptable level of detail.
2	Most of the sections of the data chart are complete with an acceptable amount of detail, or all sections complete with some errors.
1	Few of the sections are complete, or multiple errors are present.

Children's Literature Connection

Maps and Mapping

By Jinny Johnson

ISBN: 0753460629

Readers discover the world with Suki West, an adventurous cartographer. The basics of maps and map making from ancient times to today are included. Lift-up flaps and beautiful images make the book very appealing.

Maps in History

By Walter G. Olesky

ISBN: 0613595165

This book is another excellent source for the history of cartography and reproductions of old maps.

Quick Fact

Maps are really projections of what the globe would look like as a flat surface. Any such flattening distorts the size and shapes of objects. The Mercator projection, which was invented by a Flemish cartographer of that name in the 1600s, is still popular today. The problem with maps created using this projection is that land and water near the poles appear larger than comparable land and water near the equator. However, Mercator was no fool. He created his maps to be read and followed easily by the sailors of his time who were exploring the globe!

FIGURE 25.1   Exploring Maps   3rd–5th, 6th–8th

Historic Map:

  1. What do you see on this map?

  _____

  _____

  _____

  2. What symbols are used?

  _____

  _____

  _____

  3. What do you think they mean?

  _____

  _____

  _____

4. What land and water forms are on the map?

_____

_____

_____

5. What countries are named?

_____

_____

_____

6. What cities are included?

_____

_____

_____

7. What landmarks are indicated?

_____

_____

_____

Modern Map:

1. What do you see on this map?

_____

_____

_____

2. What symbols are used?

_____

_____

_____

3. What do you think they mean?

_____

_____

_____

(Continued)

FIGURE 25.1   (Continued)   3rd–5th, 6th–8th

4. What land and water forms are on the map?

_____

_____

_____

5. What countries are named?

_____

_____

_____

6. What cities are included?

_____

_____

_____

7. What landmarks are indicated?

_____

_____

_____

Compare your answers above.

How are the two maps alike?

_____

_____

_____

_____

How are the two maps different?

_____

_____

_____

_____

_____

REFERENCES

Ekiss, G. O., Trapido-Lurie, B., Phillips, J., & Hinde, E. (2007). The world in spatial terms: Mapmaking and map reading. *Social Studies and the Young Learner, 20*(2), 7–9.

National Council for the Social Studies. (1994). *Expectations of excellence: Curriculum standards for social studies.* Washington, DC: Author.

National Council of Teachers of English and International Reading Association. (1996). *Standards for the English language arts.* Urbana, IL: National Council of Teachers of English.

Selwyn, D. (1993). *Living history in the classroom: Integrative arts activities for making social studies meaningful.* Chicago: Zephyr.

About the Authors

Leah M. Melber has had the opportunity to share her excitement for social studies as an elementary classroom teacher, university professor, and natural history museum education specialist. She has focused her nearly 20 years of experience in the field of education on creating inquiry-based experience for learners of all ages. She holds a BA in zoology and an MA in education, together with a multiple-subject teaching certificate from the state of California and a PhD in educational psychology from the University of Southern California. She recently accepted a position as the Director of Student and Teacher Programs at the Lincoln Park Zoo in Chicago and is already exploring new ways to share the rich history of her institution with local school children.

Alyce Hunter has been a teacher and administrator in New Jersey's public schools for 30 years. In addition, she has been an adjunct professor in various graduate schools of education, including Rutgers University, Wagner College, Lesley University, and Centenary College. She has taught and continues to teach courses in educational leadership, literacy, and social studies education. Her doctoral degree is from Lehigh University in the field of foundations of education. Her belief that it is our responsibility and privilege as educators to nurture and honor each and every student is demonstrated in her research and writings on differentiated instruction and the connections between social studies and literacy. She has authored numerous journal articles, including most recently, an article about her high school district's one-book literacy club project, which appeared in *Principal Leadership* (May 2009). Four coauthored books on educational topics, such as mentoring, differentiated instruction, and teacher portfolios, are also to her credit.

CPSIA information can be obtained
at www.ICGtesting.com
Printed in the USA
BVHW060129270821
615174BV00006B/78

9 781412 971102